Disembodying Women

Disembodying Women

Perspectives on Pregnancy and the Unborn

Barbara Duden

Translated by Lee Hoinacki

Harvard University Press
Cambridge, Massachusetts
London, England
1993

First published as *Der Frauenleib als öffentlicher Ort: Vom Missbrauch des Begriffs Leben.*
Copyright © 1991 Luchterhand Literaturverlag GmbH.

This book is printed on acid-free paper, and its binding materials have been chosen
for strength and durability.

Library of Congress Cataloging-in-Publication Data

Duden, Barbara.
    [Frauenleib als öffentlicher Ort. English]
    Disembodying women: perspectives on pregnancy and the unborn /
    Barbara Duden; translated by Lee Hoinacki.
        p.   cm.
    Includes bibliographical references and index.
    ISBN 0-674-21267-3 (acid-free paper)
    1. Pregnant women—Public opinion—History—20th century.
    2. Pregnancy—Moral and ethical aspects. 3. Pregnancy—Social aspects.
    4. Unborn children (Law) 5. Body, Human—Social aspects. I. Title.
RG560.D3813 1993
305.4—dc20
93-17478
        CIP

Contents

How is the little creature (*kryatura*) in the belly of its mother? Let your mind imagine that the *kryatura*, being inside the belly of its mother, can be likened to a twig doubled in half. And some say like a walnut which lies inside a watery skin, with its two hands resting on its breasts, the elbows of its arms lying on its two knees, its two heels drawn up under its backside, its head also on its knees, the mouth closed, the umbilical cord open, since through this it eats what its mother eats and drinks what its mother drinks. And there is no discharge from its body, for otherwise it would kill its mother. And when it is born, what was closed is opened, what was open is closed, for if it were not thus it could not remain living for even an hour. And it has a burning candle near its head, and it sees from one corner of the world to the other, all the while being in the belly of its mother. And in all the life of that person, it never enjoys better days than those.

From *ME'AM LO'EZ,* a Sephardic Jewish
commentary on Genesis
published in Istanbul in 1730

Introduction

꩜ A PUBLIC BATTLE is under way in Germany in which both women and the churches are involved, Lutherans as deeply as Catholics. In a common declaration in 1980, these churches defined the issue as one of "future mothers," "pregnant women," "conflicts of conscience," and "the claims and rights of fathers to the birth of a child." Pregnancy and women at risk stood at the center of the discussion. By 1990, however, in a second joint statement, the tone had profoundly changed. In the interim, Presbyterians, the Salvation Army, and other groups had joined the bishops. The second statement is entitled *God Is a Friend of Life,* and in it women are eclipsed by something entirely new—*life*. "We stand in need of a joint and embracing effort by everyone for the protection of life," reads the text. "Therefore this declaration deals with the challenges and tasks involved in the protection of earth as a living space and in the protection of human life." Life, "a complex eco-system like a forest, the self-development and transmission of genetic information by a single organism, or the full development of a human being from the fertilized egg cell to the newborn and its further growth."[1]

In April 1991, 141 cardinals were called to Rome and put to work on a declaration for the protection of human life. The Pope opened the assembly by quoting from the "Exultet, iam angelica turba coelorum," a solemn hymn of jubilation that is sung in a pre-Gregorian tone when the Easter candle is blessed on Holy Saturday night. In beautiful Latin, it describes the struggle of the Redeemer with the forces of evil: "mors et vita duello conflixere mirando"—"death and life are involved in a momentous conflict." These are the words John Paul II used to open the meeting.[2] During this same time, American troops returned from the Persian Gulf and General Schwartzkopf spoke at the Cathedral of St. John the Divine in New York. No wonder the Pope's words were reported by the press as a form of spiritual warmongering. In fact, they are a spiritual leader's call to government to use secular power against millions of women allegedly intent on extinguishing "lives."

In this extended essay I want to call attention to the profound consequences, for women and for society, that accompany this public dispute. Politicians and jurists, theologians and physicians are engaged in a major effort of social creation whose object is "life." As a result of this effort, a new idea has become universally accepted: just as the Blue Planet—"seen" from space—is the environment of all life, so woman is the environment of new life. Almost overnight, these beliefs have become growth industries for new professional establishments, from ecological systems engineers to bioethicists, to manage. Concurrently, the term *life* (and *a life*) has become an idol, and controversy has attached a halo to this idol that precludes its dispassionate use in ordinary discourse. This book deals with the history of this idol—the history of life not as an object but as a notion. I want to examine the conditions under which, in the course of one generation, technology along with a new discourse has transformed pregnancy into a process to be managed, the expected child into a fetus, the mother into an ecosystem, the unborn into a life, and life into a supreme value.

I am a historian. For me, this transmogrification of the unborn into part of an endangered ecosystem is a question of historical epistemology. It is a delicate question that calls for compassion and precision, both difficult to achieve in the midst of the rhetoric and confrontation directed toward the "protection of life." What enables me to examine these questions from this particular perspective is an unusual privilege I have enjoyed. Thanks to a generous personal gift from Josh Mailman, I have been able to help organize a standing conversation among half a dozen friends of Ivan Illich. Since 1986 in State College, Pennsylvania, and now in Bremen, Germany, we have spent a few months together each year, and are frequently joined by distant colleagues who come for discussions of a few days or weeks. In each place I have conducted an open house to facilitate these "living room consultations." I am not the only one to have noticed that as a result of our style of research I can stand for every sentence in this book, even though in its origin or formulation it was a gift, but I may not be able to recall either the time or the giver. In a special way this is true of my collaboration with Lee Hoinacki, whose wry wisdom enriched my argument even more than his sense of language strengthened my English. Wolfgang Sachs, one of the participants, has stated the aim of our explorations: "to search for methods for reviewing current certainties in a historical perspective." How did modern certainties come to jell? We have seen it as our task to take a second look at apparent truths. Therefore, we have excluded most of the notions Raymond Williams discusses in *Key Words*.[3] Our attention has focused on recently coined terms that are noncontroversial, such as *development, insurance, health, aid, responsibility,* and *waste*. The means to achieve health, education, and welfare are divisive, but the necessary pursuit of these goals is today unquestioned. It is within this conversation that my eyes were opened to the recent coinage of "life" and to its surprising acceptance as something real, legal, and obviously sacred.

In these inquiries into modern certainties, I have led the discussion on the history of the body. In the 1970s, women's history took me into midwifery, and midwifery into the history of perceptions that penetrate the skin. And this brought me to the social perception of the unborn. Rather suddenly, at about the same time, the unborn became "a life." I found that this term was related to the inquiries of my colleagues, who see a parallel shift in perception in the development of ecology. The historical epistemology of ecology shows that the recent importance of "life" serves as a justification for political programs and management enterprises.

My own research into seventeenth- and eighteenth-century sources, and into the graphic techniques that enabled anatomists to recognize and popularize a new view of the body's interior, will be published as a technical book in the history of science tentatively entitled *Seeing the Unborn: The Culter and the Etching Needle as Optical Devices*. The present volume collects a set of occasional papers, which came into existence as I was asked to participate in various meetings, into a narrative whole. At times I felt a bit out of place at these meetings. For example, the German association *Pro Familia* asked me to act as a historical expert to advise the professional guidance counselors whom German women are legally required to consult before getting an abortion. I was also invited to a meeting of the International Semiotic Society in Toronto whose theme was "the object," where I focused on the fetus as "objectum paradigmaticum nostri temporis," "the paradigmatic object of our time". A few months later, in San Francisco, I presented "Quickening" at the American Historical Association meeting—sandwiched between papers on the semantics of sperm and medical discourse on hysteria in nineteenth-century France. The legal and social status of the unborn is a pressing issue in many countries. In Germany, for example, a new law on abortion is being drafted. And in this connection I was asked to collect and publish my historiographic interventions.[4] Instead, I have drawn upon them to write the present essay. I wrote it to enable the nonacademic reader to listen in on a conversation among well-read and passionately interested friends.

I want to emphasize that this essay espouses none of the positions that typically appear in current controversies over life, abortion, euthanasia, genetic engineering, or the environment. It formulates no opinion on the legal regulation of abortion or on access to prenatal care, nor does it deal with the social, ethical, or medical evaluation of chemical, genetic, or surgical interventions. I limit myself to one task: to show *historically* that the human fetus, as conceptualized today, is not a creature of God or a natural fact, but an engineered construct of modern society. I shall discuss the many-layered process involved in the synthesis of this fetus, the invention of fetal norms and needs, and the pseudoscientific directives that ascribe the responsibility for the management of a life—as defined for optimal measurement and supervision—to women. Listening to my pregnant friends and reflecting as a historian, what I am deeply troubled about is this: how a woman's acceptance of this kind of fetus not only disembodies her perceptions but forces her into a nine-month clientage in which her "scientifically" defined needs for help and counsel are addressed by professionals.

There is a lot of talk today about "reproductive choice." I look at the issue from a different angle and then suggest that women *do* have a choice when they become pregnant. They can eschew the perception of pregnancy that has come into existence only in my lifetime but is now taken for granted. They can avoid giving embodied reality to managed constructs. As a society, we can learn to question the certainties that have led us into a corner where pregnancy is defined in terms of the modern fetus and then in terms of something called "life," for which we are all asked to take public responsibility.

4 DISEMBODYING WOMEN

1

The Lost Horizon

꒒ KONRAD LORENZ once wrote a book called *Man Meets Dog*.
To be more precise, the translator could have rendered the ambiguous
German title as "How Man Was Blessed with the Dog." It is the
ethologist's story about the ways the two have shaped each other. Here,
I want to tell the story of how the modern fetus and woman have
shaped each other.

I am a historian, not an ethologist. I became one out of curiosity; I
wanted to know how "woman" came about. I couldn't avoid asking
how I came to have the body that I feel as mine, the body that most of
the time seems natural to me but about which other cultures and
epochs had no inkling. Neither my grandmother, nor Queen Victoria,
nor Hildegard of Bingen, nor any goddess of antiquity felt her flesh as
I experience mine.

The X chromosome I leave to biologists, the ethology of *foemina
sapiens* to primatologists, the moment of a woman's ensoulment to
theologians, and her humanization to colleagues in women's studies.
What interests me is how women's flesh felt in earlier ages. To understand the poetry of Sappho, Christine de Pisan, or Amy Lowell, I ask
how heart and belly and hair, joy and longing and melancholy, have
been perceived in the body of woman in other times.

As for what motivated me, it is quite simple. In the words of Michel
Foucault,

It was curiosity—the only kind of curiosity, in any case, that is
worth acting upon with a degree of obstinacy: not the curiosity

that seeks to assimilate what is proper for one to know, but that which enables one to get free of oneself. After all, what would be the value of the passion for knowledge if it resulted only in a certain amount of knowledgeableness and not . . . in the knower's straying afield of himself. There are times in life when the question of knowing if one can think differently than one thinks, and perceive differently than one sees, is absolutely necessary if one is to go on looking and reflecting at all . . . But then, what is philosophy today—philosophical activity . . . if not [the] endeavor to know how and to what extent it might be possible to think differently?[1]

One who follows this curiosity soon reaches the borders of his or her discipline. In the early 1980s, then, I had to move beyond the boundaries of my department to find out about the body state of women who were long dead.

In this inquiry, my subject is not woman imagined or woman represented in the past as *Theotokos* ("God-bearer"), as mother, or as whore. Nor is it the conception, definition, and scientific construction of woman by Aristotle, Galen, Albertus Magnus, or Sigmund Freud. Those who want to read about woman as a failed man, or woman as *Theotokos,* or the "discovery" of female orgasm by American medicine and English law after 1865 can pick up a full-fledged treatise on any of these subjects. I acknowledge my gratitude to Carolyn Bynum and Marie-Christine Pouchelle, to Ludmilla Jordanova and Emily Martin, to Angus McLaren and Thomas Laqueur.[2] What I want to know is how the body we discovered as "ourselves" in the 1970s came to be, because it is this body that has become the shibboleth. And it is this very body that has been projected by innumerable "women" studies onto women long dead. As far as I know, it does not fit them.

˙ I have cut only my own small piece from a large pie. Those who want to look at the present from the perspective of ancient Greek, Roman, or paleo-Christian sources can read Giulia Sissa, Aline Rousselle, or Peter Brown, respectively.[3] I limit myself to the social construction of woman as a scientific fact, the foundations for which were laid in the eighteenth century. And I ask how this "fact" became so popular that it could be internalized and experienced by women like myself. I want to know how I came to have a hormone level whose variations I "feel," and how my friend came to have a fetus that she "sees." I was forced to ask these questions as I read eighteenth-century female patient protocols and was frustrated until I came to understand that in some of its most basic aspects the felt body of these women was not like mine.

In this essay I have to leave aside much of what I would like to say about the contrasts between the heart and skin and blood of women then and now in order to focus on pregnancy. The creature I read about in the Sephardic Jewish commentary on Genesis of 1730, *ME'AM LO'EZ,*[4] is as unlike the latter-day fetus as is the "stagnation" experienced by Lutheran women in Lower Saxony at the time the commentary was written. Thus, the theme of this book as it emerges from the historical record is not the similarity but the heteronomy in women's experience of the unborn at different points in the past and today.

My mother most emphatically insists that when she was expecting me she never thought of me as a fetus. And I remember a time when the fetus could be featured only in the kind of books that also showed labia majora and pubic hair. But now we are overwhelmed with fetuses. I encountered one recently in a German ad for a Swedish car. Another one confronted me from the top of a circular urging me to discuss abortion with my candidate before giving him my vote. A pregnant colleague who came to my office asked me to extinguish a cigarette. Why? Because she thinks that for the next six months she is the ecosystem for a fetus.

How did the unborn turn into a billboard image and how did that isolated goblin get into the limelight? How did the female peritoneum acquire transparency? What set of circumstances made the skinning of woman acceptable and inspired public concern for what happens in her innards? And, finally, the embarrassing question: how was it possible to mobilize so many women as uncomplaining agents of this skinning and as willing witnesses to the creation of this haunting symbol of loneliness?[5] To explore these questions we must do two things: First, we must find words and images and a way of presentation that allows a modern reader to grasp how unseen beings were present in other times. Then we must strive to keep the argument outside the large shadow cast by the fiery rhetoric of the abortion debate.

For a decade I have searched for methods of dealing with the historical experience of the physical self that lies beneath the skin, and for obvious reasons I have privileged women in my research. I have sought accounts revealing their experience in diaries, medical records, complaints registered in literature, letters, and statements to a doctor, all written after 1650. I have noted everything that would tell me about the self known by touch, kinesthetic perception, and synesthetic experience and tried to make sense of what I read. It was inevitable that this interest in gut perceptions would lead me to pregnancy as a high point of such carnal knowledge. With much hesitation, but urged on by curiosity, I have tried to write the history of what until recently was felt but never seen. Because I was concentrating on pregnancy, this became the historiography of what women, and only women, can touch.[6]

ˠ The further I went into a history of the body—that is, a history of the female body—the more clearly I saw that there are two stories to be told. One is the story of what can be seen by physicians, artists, and women themselves. It deals with woman as her flesh and being is, or can be, exposed to the gaze. More subtly, it is the story of what can be imagined as long as we keep to the sense of image as that which *could* be seen. The other is the story of touch and vision, which grope in the darkness beneath the skin. When one of us goes to a medical clinic, she usually has something wrong and can describe it as something that *is*. In contrast, those distant women I have tried to approach come to the physician and tell him what has *happened* to them. They report on events that come at them from the outside or go on within them. At first I thought this was only a different use of grammar, but soon I recognized that in those days women suffered from experiences that have lost all meaning for us. They report on an "ebbing" and "flowing" and "curdling" and "hardening" and, above all, on an interior orientation of their being that is mysterious today but which in their own time was immediately understandable, not only to other women, but also to the physician. Forced to see, to represent, to imagine, we have a restricted sensorium for the invisible shapes inside us. The Enlightenment has removed from our bellies, as from our minds, any reality that is not perceived by the eye. Body history, as I have come to recognize, is to a large extent a history of the unseen. Until very recently, the unborn, by definition, was one of these.

It would be a mistake to say that historians have completely neglected the invisible. True, when we think of history's objects the first things that come to mind are ruins and roads, kings and knights, or abstractions of behavior that we classify as customs, *mentalités*, ideas, ideologies, or laws. But the invisible has also found its historians. In fact, one of the major events in recent historiography has been the inclusion of invisible beings in the list of subjects that can be legitimately dealt with by the discipline: the dead who appear as ghosts, visions, and spooks; saints or ancestors; angels, nature spirits, and gods. Without knowing the habits ascribed to saints, it would be difficult to explore the foundation of many European cities or to discover why major roads run from Poland and Hungary through southern Germany and on to one of two passes across the Pyrenees to Santiago de Campostella. Angels have intervened in battles and in one decided the issue with lightning. People saw angels for generations and felt themselves safe in the shadow of their wings. But not all elementary spirits are as personable as the kobolds and salamanders and melusines that were described by the Swiss physician Paracelsus in the sixteenth century. And students of folk culture and chemistry alike are familiar with their historical status.

Above all, there has never been a community that did not cohabit with its dead. But today, socially, the dead are no more. They are deceased. They are ontic has-beens. And with the vanishing of the dead, the most significant distinction between *homo* and all other primates is gone. When you show me a paleolithic skull, I recognize it as human not because of the cubic measure of the brain or because of the hand tools found in the grave but because of the signs of burial. These reveal that this "person" lived a life on the borderline between the seen and the unseen, in the presence of the living and the dead. Neither the dead nor other invisible beings had to show themselves to be considered social realities.

In spite of the degree to which the invisible impinged on events, these beings were not considered a legitimate subject for historians. In earlier times they appeared in history books as superstitious ideas or ancient illusions. More recently, this has changed. Now, competent historical monographs deal with the history of angels, the Devil, the dead, God the Father in art, and the souls in Purgatory. But one invisible entity has so far remained outside the scope of historians. For some strange reason, no one has written a history of the unborn.

And yet, among the invisible, the unborn, which is invisible in the body of a woman, is an important historical subject. Two things distinguish it from others of its kind. It is never there with certainty. In spite of many signs and intimations of its presence, one can never be sure about it. Unlike the dead, one's guardian angel, or God, it cannot be grasped by faith; it remains a hope. And second, before a child comes to light it is a *nondum,* a "not-yet." It has a peculiar temporal dimension. It is the only one of the invisible beings that knocks at the door of existence and emerges as an infant.

It has become very difficult for us today to realize, to sense, the horizon beyond which the not-yet was hidden for most of historical time. One of the most fundamental but least noted events in the second half of the twentieth century is the loss of horizon. We live somewhere between satellite TV, which knows no skyline, and the telephone, which allows us to reach beyond our line of vision to connect with any number we choose. It requires a special effort to remember that there ever was a horizon, although it has only recently been erased. It was just yesterday that the whole earth suddenly "appeared" as the Blue Planet and we began to accept the fact that all would be exposed to recording equipment orbiting far above this Tower of Babel. I regard the fetus as one of the modern results of living without a horizon.

Thus, the unborn is an invisible being with multiple claims to history. It is closely tied to the history of hope. But when hope is dissolved into expectations that can be managed at will, scientifically, sociologically, and arbitrarily, the unborn is no more. Its history is tied to the history of the body. Once it was a hoped-for child that might emerge from below the horizon. But overnight it has been transformed into a unique immune system in real time.

2

The Nilsson Effect

ᔓᕗ ON NEW YORK'S Fifth Avenue, opposite Saks, a man is selling back issues of *Life* magazine. I buy those appearing in April 1965. On April 2, the cover shows *Gemini* and "the lift-off to a new era in space," on April 16, the pilot of a helicopter-gunship over Vietnam. April 23 features Frank Sinatra. The snippets of world history pasted together in *Life* bring back the mood of the mid-sixties. April 30 shows "the drama of life before birth . . . An unprecedented photographic feat in color . . . A living eighteen-week-old fetus shown inside its amniotic sac is seen at the right."[1]

I look at the figure in its transparent balloon, the limbs drawn up to the torso. A background appears, like a starry sky. A glossy umbilical cord connects the creature to a pink bubbly shape, and I am reminded of photos of astronauts floating in space. Next comes a picture showing the "competition" of the sperm for the egg:

> . . . millions of sperm and only one egg. The birth of human life really occurs at the moment the mother's egg cell is fertilized by one of the father's sperm cells . . . the male sperm as they enter the cervix are affected by the presence of the egg. If there is no prospect of an egg, they just mill around aimlessly, as at left . . . But while an egg is present . . . they stream purposefully toward it. Swimming upstream, by lashing their tails back and forth, they move at a rate of three inches per hour across the cervix, through the uterus and up the fallopian tube to meet the egg.[2]

I go to Forty-second Street and ask for a current issue of *Life*—it is August 1990. I open it and place the two issues, separated by twenty-five years, next to one another. Each shows the style and substance of its respective time, inextricably fused.

In both subtlety and depth, the differences between the two issues are striking. In the 1990 issue I read:

> . . . the first pictures ever of how life begins . . . The first days of Creation . . . a chronicle of human development from its first second through its earliest hours and days.[3]

The first difference touches upon the relationship between the picture and the corresponding text. In 1965, the pictures could still be taken as illustrations of an extended caption. They gave the reader a more explicit image of what was being said in so many words. Looking up from a sentence, the reader might have said, "Aha, sperm look like elongated tadpoles!" When he moved from the words to the photograph, he would project into the color picture the shapes or figures or entities he had learned to recognize. The *Life* photographer, Lennart Nilsson, still conceived of himself as a descendant of the copper engraver, who in the sixteenth century had made illustration possible, and the wood engraver or lithographer, who in the nineteenth century had made it cheap and therefore popular.

By 1990 the illustrative function of the picture has been inverted. In this issue, the pictures confront the onlooker with a cloudy chimera for which one has no simile. Without instructions from the writer, one cannot read anything into these shapes. Nothing seen, perhaps nothing ever dreamt, gives a clue to what has been photographed here. The text in 1990 is further from one's experience than that in 1965, but the sentences are more apodictic. We are told what to see; we are told that these clouds and masses were recorded by a scanning ultramicroscope *and* that they represent a human being. Our readiness to see *on command* has grown tremendously in the intervening twenty-five years.

I see a greenish-golden disk in a violet field to which, on the left side, some yellowish bubbles are attached. These form a cloudlike shape from which a sulfurous fog emanates. I read (1990 text):

> Two hours. Like an eerie planet floating through space, a woman's egg or ovum (above left) has been ejected by one of her ovaries

into a fallopian tube . . . The luminous halo around the ovum is a cluster of nutrient cells feeding the hungry egg.

On the next page I see a jagged, rocky, reddish expanse. In it, upright, a disk in a golden glow. The disk itself is brown and yellow, and its edges a metallic green. It has a granular veneer upon which two much smaller bumpy circles appear:

> Now that the head of the sperm has entered the ovum, there are two small bubbles filled with chromosomes floating around (opposite top), one from the woman and one from the man . . . drawn inexorably toward each other, [they] soon meet . . . The result is a single nucleus that contains an entire biological blueprint for a new individual, genetic information governing everything from the length of the nose to the diseases that will be inherited. About twelve hours later the cell begins its incredible nine-month journey by taking the first step . . . down the fallopian tube toward the uterus.

On the next page, the caption says:

> Two days . . . the blastocyst is attempting to pass through the narrowest opening of the fallopian tube just before entering the uterus. The space is so restricted the embryo can barely jostle and squeeze its way through.

Turning the page, I see a planetlike bubble floating above the landscape. Four square insets show the bubble in three stages of eruption. The caption says:

> Four days. Gliding into the uterus, the blastocyst (right) . . . bounces along the uterine wall (opposite) . . . feeling its way for a comfortable home to spend the next 39 weeks . . . Although now free to attach itself anywhere, the blastocyst is picky and may take as many as three days to decide on a spot, usually near the uterine ceiling.

On the following page I see an enormous brownish, crackled lump composed of overlapping lobes against a strange background. The caption says:

Eight days. The blastocyst has landed! Like a lunar module, the embryo facilitates its landing on the uterus with leg-like structures composed of sugar molecules on the surface.

In an interview printed in the German *(Stern)* edition, Nilsson, the photographer, comments on this shot:

> Just a few moments ago there was nothing but a free-floating mass of cells . . . Now communication has been established. The antibodies of the pregnant woman withdraw. "We are accepted, we may stay!" It is a human being, one hundred percent.[4]

In marked contrast are the photographs taken in 1965, which have since become part of the mental universe of our time. They show the unfinished child looking like an astronaut in its transparent bubble, a bluish-pink figure with protruding veins sucking its thumb, the vaguely human face with closed eyes covered by a tissue veil. The fetus shown in the photographs was removed from a dead woman or a tubal pregnancy. The "beginning of life" sequence Nilsson sold to the press and the textbook publishers showed mainly corpses. Live observation was still a largely unrealized prospect.

Even in 1965 some photographs were taken *in situ,* but the fiber optics needed for fetoscopy were still in an early stage of development. A wide-angle lens was attached to a light source and mounted on one end of a flexible bundle of fiberglass that could be pushed through the cervix. This apparatus provided pictures of segments within the uterus so small that they made sense only if a number of them were mounted and retouched in a photographic lab and made into "a picture." The result was a little hand or foot. This popular exhibition of fetoscopy spoke powerfully about the desire to dissolve the frontier between the viewer's eye and the unborn. It effected the breakdown of a horizon which, since the beginning of history, had made the unborn an unseen and unverifiable presence. But the instruments were still inadequate and the frontier over which they were meant to trespass was still formidable.

If we analyze its function, the image of the fetus in the 1960s was a constructed object comparable to portrait or nude photography. Like them, it invited the viewer to admire the photographer's art in revealing what the naked eye could see but would not easily notice. The stuff shown was still in the order of the visible, although this particular view of it required the intervention of an artist and his technical equipment. Fetoscopy, on the other hand, solicited the viewer to join in an immodest adventure like a peeping Tom.

The *Life* magazine of 1965 panders to the *libido videndi*, the ravenous urge to extend one's sight, to see more, to see things larger or smaller than the eye can grasp—to see things which have previously been off limits. In these now dated photographs the object is something that can show itself to the onlooker. They are pictures whose interpretation and understanding is left to a large extent to the viewer, whose experience equips her to see something when she examines them.

When I say that I "see," I always imply that I have seen *something,* a substance. In this sense, a camera does not see. My glance is a human act only when I see a substance that I interpret as something meaningful to me. When light is reflected by the surface of skin and hair, I know that I see a certain person. I look at a face and I see you. Seeing is always the synthesis of an optical impact on the retina that initiates certain nerve reactions and elicits a set of preconceptions. Thus, human sight is an art that must be learned, but it can be aided by technique. Optical devices can extend sight. Leeuwenhoek, the man who "invented" the microscope, ground 419 lenses, some smaller than a pinhead, to arrive at a two-hundredfold enlargement, until finally one day in 1676 in Delft, he saw the "little seed animals," the *animalcula seminalia*. He saw what nobody before him had seen because he had learned how to disperse and redirect the rays of the sun.[5] For the next few decades, the tadpoles Leeuwenhoek had seen were believed to be testicular parasites, which kept the seminal fluid liquid and warm. Only toward the end of that century was it "recognized" that the head of the spermatozoon contained human "pollen" that dissolved in the egg, thus fertilizing it. The genes that are "really" there, and that are shown today, are something that cannot be *seen.* Shadows can be shown, but they stand for substance only insofar as the onlooker takes the caption on faith and accepts what she is told, what she must "see."

Faith is the substance of things unseen (Rom. 10:17). By faith, we hold as true those things that can in no way be visualized. But one cannot see all things that can be visualized in the same light. This is a statement that was firmly held by philosophers and theologians and subscribed to by popular culture long before the invisible parts of the electromagnetic spectrum were known. A difference was recognized between those things that can be seen by the light of the sun or the flame of a candle and those things that can show themselves on rare occasions without losing their status as members of a class of invisible beings. Some such visions may be everyday occurrences. Others are exceptions—some dreaded, some desired.

The lust of the eye has been recognized by all great traditions as a delightful though dangerous propensity that, for the sake of deep and artful enjoyment, must submit to a certain disciplinary custody. But this zestful, sometimes prurient, always distracting craving to feed on sights has traditionally been distinguished from the invocation and evocation of invisible hosts. Ghosts, summoning the dead, interpreting omens, possession, and entering into visions of the future, the distant, and the otherworldly tend to be clearly distinguished from things seen in the light of the sun, moon, or fire. Disciplined reflection upon these varied categories of the visionary shows that they have something in common: they are invisible entities that can show themselves, that can be invited or even forced to appear.

Historians have dedicated monographs to the lust of the eye and to the history of visions, dreams, and appearances. But so far they have not honored the contributions made by philosophers and pheno-menologists who have recognized that the new trend toward vision on command must be contrasted not only with the traditional history of sight, but also with that of vision as shaped by culture and art. When I contrast the *Life* of 1965 with the *Life* of 1990 on this deeper level, I recognize that the first is still strongly on the side of the representation of the visible, the second mainly concerned with the depiction of things that lie beyond the eye's horizon, which, to be "seen," must be ex-plained by some authority.

There is nothing new about the depiction of invisible entities: the great spirit of the hunt in the cave at Lascaux, God the Father with a beard, or pictures of angels are random examples. For the last couple of centuries, representations of the invisible have often been discussed as artistic projections of subjective or collective visualizations in dreams or under the influence of drugs. What makes the recent issue of *Life* so typical of a new kind of seeing is the disappearance of the frontier between visible things that are visibly re-presented and invis-ible things to which representation imputes visibility.

In 1965, the line between the picture that shows resemblance and the picture that represents an abstract notion still held. That line has now eroded, due partly to trivialization by technological devices: TV was then half as old as it is today. People still did not accept that what they knew as an event was mainly the creation of the media; visible PR in politics still turned people off rather than on. The earth was not yet the Blue Planet, that is, a media event turned, via Spaceship Earth, into Gaia, the subject of an elegant mathematical theory. War correspondents showed maimed soldiers and the dead rather than missions photographed through cross hairs. On all these points, the *Life* magazine of 1990 speaks out of a different milieu. Increasingly, the managed image has become the precondition for sight: the sunset has become as beautiful as a picture postcard.

For years I lived in a divided city, Berlin. The Wall was up, and we knew in our guts where the frontier lay. When I want to speak about the fading distinction between the seen and the shown, about the disappearance of skin that in 1965 still divided the inside of the body from the outside of the body as we experience it, I have an easy time when I address fellow Berliners. I can simply call their attention to what has happened since November 1989. For thirty years there was the Wall. "This side" and "over there" were two realms of reality; no one really believed they were just the result of a wall. Then the Wall came down, and none of us can fully avoid a sense of physical discomfort when we notice that even its traces have disappeared. Something like this has happened to the frontier between what is seen and what is shown. And the distinction between the unquestionably visible and that which is shown to me in fascinating "concreteness" is not just gone; in many instances it has left no traces.

Now, we see what we are shown. We have gotten used to being shown no matter what, within or beyond the limited range of human sight. This habituation to the monopoly of visualization-on-command strongly suggests that only those things that can in some way be visualized, recorded, and replayed at will are part of reality. Starting with children's TV and prekindergarten videos, new generations are being socialized to see whatever appears on the screen. We have all been trained to live by the recognition of flash cards, news bites, spots, ads, digests, catalogues, schedules, or class hours. Each of these packages is a bundle of lures that inveigles a side of reality which beguiles us as something we must be told about because we cannot see it on our own. The result is a strange mistrust of our own eyes, a disposition to take as real only that which is mechanically displayed in a photograph, a statistical curve, or a table. Eyewitness testimony must be "substantiated" by records that have been acquired, and can be stored and then shown.

The objects of the first days after conception exhibited in *Life* in 1990 are by their very nature invisible. The surface of the blastocyst landing on the uterine mucus "shows" features that are much smaller than the wavelength of violet light. Sugar molecules cannot be illuminated for the photographer. The object which appears on the emulsion is of an order of magnitude that makes it unfit to reflect light. What we see on the page is a collage of digital measurements made by the interference of electron bundles with molecules. It is a misnomer to call this photo-*graphy*, which means drawing done by light. What we see is photo-*geny*, an appearance concocted by the use of light.

In 1990 Nilsson uses a laboratory tool, the electron microscope, not to verify a biological theory but to create a semblance of natural science representing his own visualization of "the beginning of a human life." The theory visualized posits the scientific proposition that the nuclear substance found in the object scanned by the electron bundles is not homogeneous with the nuclear substance found in the other cells that make up the organism of the maternal "landing pad." But the heterogeneity between the chromosomes of the reproducer and the reproduced is not what this particular experiment demonstrates. That is verified by completely different laboratory procedures. The genetic heterogeneity of the "module" and its "landing surface" cannot be read out of the results of this scan, much less "seen" in *Life*. It is an assumption based on previous studies made by biologists when they use an electron microscope to observe a stage in the evolution of these cells. Nilsson would not be a bit less convincing if he had used the results of scanning ultramicroscopy on tissues of any other species. In fact, exactly the same statement can be made about thousands of other species that do not inspire Nilsson's artistic endeavor. A biologist's statement that this is genetic material from the species *homo* has none of the significance and meaning implied in the caption, which refers to the picture as "a human life." And the sequence from zygote to viable baby appears in the same issue that contains new candid shots of John F. Kennedy from his birth to his death in Dallas. What concerns me here is the iconic power of these visual statements within our culture. I believe that they reinforce our training to dissociate vision from sight in a very special way.

Jewish myth tells of the intercourse between humans and the sons of gods that was customary before the Flood, when humans were equipped with different eyes. Then, the daughters of men could see the sons of gods. But after the Flood the range of human sight was restricted. The Creator made a pact with Noah: He promised never again to destroy the earth by water. But that pact was concluded under a meaningful sign, the rainbow arc that spans the visible spectrum from one end to the other and rests at the boundaries—violet and red—of the invisible. Within this span of colors, man was given sight in order to marvel, to enjoy, to inquire, and to lust. Beyond lay the realm forbidden to sight, the eerie domain where necromancers dabble and the region of mysteries that cannot be seen by the rays of the sun, which He reveals only to prophets. That is how the story goes. Losing a real horizon, we have lost this sense of obscurity. Through immodest revelations—for example, the skinning of woman's body—we have lost the power to discriminate between the seen and the shown. We have gotten used to a world of confused figments where, for a churchman, a vague clump is a persuasive argument for "a life made in the image and likeness of God." The Great Potter's clay has been turned into a montage programmed by a genetic code.

If ever there was an age that began on one day, then, according to Roland Barthes, it was the modern age.[6] And that day was June 7, 1831, when the outline of the house across the street appeared on a silver-coated copper plate treated with iodine vapor by Nicéphore Niépce in Louis Jacques Daguerre's studio. It was the first lasting heliography, a design made by the sun at man's request but without the mediation of a painter's brain or hand. Since then, we have been swamped by the descendants of daguerreotypes. Even a poor man can now look upon his ancestors. Science has increasingly become the analysis of photographs. Because of growing technical refinement, the population of known stars doubles every nine years. Politics has been taken over by the media; Trotsky was "disappeared" from a politburo group photo. UFOs are first photographed and then debunked as visual tricks. Yet photographs under plastic create identity. They validate observation in the courts, the labs, and the news. "Photographs furnish evidence," says Susan Sontag.[7]

Photographs also broaden their power to give "proof" for the invisible. Once a confirmation or a clue for visual memory, they now place the invisible before the eye. This shift, too, can be demonstrated by comparing the two issues of *Life*. In the gutsy race of the sperm in 1965, the public is shown a polished version of what the microscopist has actually seen under his lenses. What is shown is the image and likeness of an optical phenomenon that can be observed. This is no longer true in 1990. The later prints show a digital collage of measurements that stand for something which can never leave the realm of darkness that is beyond violet light.

I would never suggest a causal relationship between photographic technique and the social trend toward misplaced concreteness. *Life* does not sell because readers want to contemplate moon rocks or their equivalent, or uterine molecules, but because these images satisfy their pining for breakthroughs. Without limits given by horizon and darkness, the gaze cannot come to rest, it loses its power to generate a place. Instead of finding satisfaction in the momentary sensual balance that comes from squinting, turning the head, and straining on tiptoe to focus for a glimpse of someone who is passing, the eye emptily waits for the next item brought in from the beyond. This sight-simulating stare is the viewer's contribution to the virtual reality the media create.

The urge to extend sight led to the eyeglasses that first appeared in paintings in the sixteenth century and to Galileo's fourth telescope, which made visible the moons of Jupiter and the mountains on our moon. It also led to knowledge of the stellar nature of the Andromeda nebula. It allowed late-seventeenth-century English ladies meeting for tea to explore new surfaces that, under the microscope, exploded to reveal unsuspected sights: pores of skin and wood, of flies, bees, and moths. But with photography, a page in the history of the gaze was turned. Without straining a muscle, without squinting or turning, without having to choose the focus or frame or subject, a mechanical/chemical process generates a two-dimensional pattern from which the eye is challenged to construct "a sight."

This powerful trend toward misplaced concreteness is the result of intensive, albeit informal, training. Our culture leads us into the habit of indiscriminately bestowing the status of reality on the visual appearances of Kennedy, Blue Planet, Kuwait, Madonna, or zygote, while touch, taste, proprio-ception, smell, and hetero-ception are lumped together as *impressions*. Increasingly, modern images suffice to establish the other's existence, even his presence. This makes it easier to understand how an editor can simply expect *Life*'s readers to recognize "a life" in Nilsson's collages. From top to bottom, our society has become addicted to what might be called a visual command performance.

The Vatican official in charge of the office formerly held by the Grand Inquisitor provides a good instance of this confusion between sight and appearance. In the "Instruction on Respect for Human Life in Its Origins and on the Dignity of Procreation," released on the Feast of St. Peter's Chair, 1987, Cardinal Ratzinger does not hesitate to use the latest embryological terminology to provide further confirmation of the Magisterium's teaching on procured abortion. In this auxiliary, supporting argument, he demands that Catholics recognize that "right from fertilization is begun the adventure of a human life."[8] He is accepting a definition from the current frame of a natural science, investing the object so defined with moral and religious significance and attributing to this object the status of a person. He argues that the mere *appearance* of the scientific fact leads one to the recognition of a personal presence. His position is stated with great subtlety:

> Certainly no experimental datum can be in itself sufficient to bring us to the recognition of a spiritual soul; nevertheless, the conclusions of science regarding the human embryo provide a valuable indication for discerning by the use of reason a personal presence at the moment of this first appearance of a human life: How could a human individual not be a human person? The Magisterium has not expressly committed itself to an affirmation of a philosophical nature, but it constantly reaffirms the moral condemnation of any kind of procured abortion. This teaching has not been changed and is unchangeable.[9]

Although careful qualifications have been made, the overall assurance in the acceptance of scientific "facts" and the powers of reason make one question the character of this kind of presentation. And for historians of nineteenth-century Germany, this argument has a familiar ring. At the First Vatican Council in 1868, German bishops were among the minority who tried to avoid the use of precisely such words. A conciliar decree was then being framed making it into a dogma that man "by the natural light of human reason can with certainty recognize the existence of the creator from his creatures."[10] The above-mentioned "Instruction" of 1987 is not backed by the authority of an

Ecumenical Council, nor does it teach—like the document of 1870—that human reason can "with certainty" recognize a personal presence in a biological fact. Surprisingly, however, current papal teaching derives its theological authority from a philosophical argument that in turn rests on observations which are scientifically and instrumentally engendered facts. I am not here concerned with the political or ethical consequences that result from this orientation but with the evidence it furnishes for the current transformation of a scientific fact into an emblematic appearance that is then treated as a personal presence.

This trend toward the personalization of technogenic appearance shows up even more clearly at the end of the "Instruction on Respect for Human Life." The conclusion takes the form of an "invitation" addressed to the faithful and to non-Christians alike:

> In the light of the truth about the gift of human life and in the light of the moral principles which flow from that truth, everyone is invited to act in the area of responsibility proper to each and, like the Good Samaritan, recognize as a neighbor even the littlest among the children of men (Lk. 10.29–37). Here Christ's words find a new and particular echo: "What you do to one of the least of my brethren, you do unto me" (Mt. 25.40).[11]

What does this mean? Alluding to a scientific fact (the unique genetic program in the DNA of the zygote) that can be verified only under laboratory conditions and properly formulated only in technical terminology, and perhaps influenced by the fascinating collages that helped to popularize and ideologize these cells, the Vatican Secretariat calls upon everyone, regardless of their faith, to recognize a brother in an invisible unborn without face or hands.

This kind of statement comes as a surprise to anyone acquainted with the writings of Cardinal Ratzinger when he was a theology professor. In a book on Christian brotherhood published in 1966, he stated that

> in our analysis . . . Jesus did not describe everyone as his brothers and sisters but only those who were one with him in their assent to the will of the father . . . Only in this limited application the idea of brotherhood is Christian; removal of this barrier was an essential unrealizable ideal of the Enlightenment . . . It is only

participation in the eucharistic liturgical assembly that makes a person a true member of the Christian fraternal community.[12]

The statement about the zygote as a brother could be interpreted as an error by a theologian now employed as a top-level ecclesiastical bureaucrat, or as the conversion of the anti-modernist Roman Church to "modern genetic science [which] brings valuable confirmation,"[13] or as a symptom of the degree to which concreteness, mistakenly attributed to appearances, has become an accepted part of the age's overarching certainties. This last possibility would be the most significant for an understanding of our time. It would mean that the only major institution which claims direct roots in antiquity now bows to the misplacement of personhood by interpreting a digitalized shadow, tattooed according to geneticists by a unique numerical code, as demanding "the unconditional respect that is morally due to the human being in his bodily and spiritual totality."[14]

In quoting this decree, it is not my intention to involve the reader in theological reflection, but to interpret a document that is of historical significance for our time. The cultures that have grown from Roman and Byzantine roots have a uniquely ambiguous relationship to the flesh because of the Christian belief that the biblical God was truly enfleshed and born of Mary. Like it or not, this faith in the fleshly, bloody presence of God as man has been a determining motif for war and architecture, for laws and executions, for poetry and martyrdom for over two thousand years. The uniquely Western public concern for the sick, the hungry, and the destitute has grown out of the belief that Christians can recognize in their flesh the Son of God made man. It was not the Enlightenment that introduced the unrealizable idea of institutionalizing and depersonalizing Christian love of neighbor by transforming it into the professional care of strangers. A thousand years earlier, the Church had launched the West into the business of providing welfare and relief, offering care as a mask for burnt-out love. In spite of this historical leadership in the transformation of a personal and shocking encounter between a Palestinian—then called Samaritan—and a mugged Jew into institutions created for the care of people defined by the abstract category in which they are placed, for the historian the new leadership provided by Rome remains surprising. The Vatican uses the parable of the Samaritan (Luke 10:25–37) as a justification for the Church's novel demand that "brotherly love" be extended to a faceless and shapeless appearance on the screen, the reality of which is established only by its being a scientific fact.

The meaning of the Incarnation—enfleshment—and the meaning of eyewitness are subverted as a result. Flesh has become untouchable, the whole person invisible. Finally, "love of neighbor," which through the coldness of faith in the Christian community led toward increasing institutionalization and the care of strangers, now moves one step further into the abstract.

3

The Average Fetus in Harlem

A WOMAN might possibly object to being viewed as a container for someone's brother, but it seems clearly destructive of her own sense of being alive to have her insides registered by a demographer and then to have a graphic artist make the statistical abstraction real.

Lennart Nilsson's 1990 pictures generate a persuasive illusion. They assemble in visual form digital measurements of an object that cannot be perceived by the senses. The result is a misplaced concreteness. The complementary technique of visualization achieves just the opposite. Certain graphics convincingly create the illusion that abstract notions have a tangible reality. The *Life* photos of 1965 give the fetus an aura of bodily presence. Graphs in a newspaper advertise the rationality of an "objective" view. Nilsson's paleo-baby elicits sympathy. A graph that correlates genes with biographic probabilities reduces destiny to a biological supposition and Providence to a theory of hereditary endowment. The fetus, when placed on a graph, implies status, chance, risk, and incidence rates; it suggests the future life of a gamesman. Each prenatal visit to the clinic serves as a training session for the forthcoming game.

On a recent visit to Harlem, I had an opportunity to observe how far we have gone in the didactics through which flesh is reduced to data. I was taken to a prenatal center near One-hundred-and-fortieth Street, an area where Puerto Ricans replaced the black population some time ago. Now, wretched refugees from less privileged parts of the Caribbean are pouring in. When we arrived at the storefront clinic, we found small desks, barely shielded from one another by tattered screens. At each one, an interview was taking place. I accompanied a sociologist doing research on the motives that brought women to the clinic. Advertisements, the radio, and home visitor referrals were each a factor, but in her opinion, most came because they felt lost when pregnant in New York City and because they wanted to explore welfare opportunities. One word seemed to dominate the conversation, *"Mire!,"* which means "Look!" I wondered about what there was to be seen.

Having obtained permission from the woman being interviewed, we joined one of the sessions. From her dress, demeanor, and way of speaking, it was clear that the counselor was from New York itself, while the client was a very recent arrival who might have become pregnant before leaving the island. She had come at the urging of a welfare worker and seemed to accept the visit as part of pregnancy in the United States. In fact, however, a foundation finances this city-run unit. Taking more than one hour with each woman, the interviewer seeks to make prenatal tests attractive to the client and to motivate her to give "informed" consent to still unspecified procedures. Suddenly, goose pimples appeared on my arms. Upset, I realized that we three professionals had begun the work of actually skinning this woman, a process that not only violated her bodily integrity, but also sought to deflower her spirit.

But ironically, I was impressed by the empathy of the counselor for Maria Sanchez (not her real name). When practical questions about further prenatal arrangements came up, I noticed that she was especially considerate. She did not just hand Maria one of the printed flyers, she also wrote a note about subway connections on one sheet and underlined the office hours on another. The "business" part of the exchange between the two women, however, was in sharp contrast to this chatty advice. Seated behind the desk, I could "look" for myself. *"Mire!"* The counselor pointed out the curve on a diagram that showed the statistical risk of malformed children for New York mothers older than thirty-five. Did Maria grasp that her age was being made into an issue? I could see that the graph left her confused. This is her sixth pregnancy. She has four children and seven siblings. Her mother told her that the older the mother the brighter the child. And who could deny that the daughters of older women remain young into the ad-vanced age of their mothers? The counselor's insistence on risk made little sense to Maria. The thick circle the counselor penciled far down on the bell-shaped curve did not touch her.

The day before, I had been taken for a long visit to a home in that neighborhood. While there I was surprised that there were three interruptions within a few hours by people making rounds and ringing doorbells. One was selling insurance, a Jehovah's Witness wanted to discuss the Bible, and a third man offered a VCR on monthly installments. Now, as I looked at Maria, I thought of my previous day's experience. Like the woman in that household, Maria, too, seemed unwilling to buy. As she sat here, she was urged to accept a fetus. She was being bombarded with a dozen notions that together make up the conceptual framework of a slum pregnancy in New York: normal development, risk, expectancy, fetus, social security payments, and the like. Although I consciously refrain from questioning the medical and social effectiveness of these controls because my theme is the symbolic result of the procedures, what I am trying to understand is the difference the encounter with a professional makes for Maria and the degree to which it removes her from the way her mother experienced the body. Maria is given a graphic representation of something called a typical fetus, which assumes the notion of normality expressed in measurements, such as average weight and position. Maria must stretch her imagination to grasp these abstractions. The experience of her mother was more sensual, warm, touchable, familiar.

When this sort of question is raised in a medical milieu, it usually leads to a call for better preparation of the counselor, so that she can inspire confidence in the benefits of these procedures. My point is that the procedures *themselves* must be questioned, not, however, from the perspective of their technical efficacy but from that of their inevitable psychic results. What do they do to the woman's self-understanding? Actually, the better the counseling, the more authoritatively convincing are certain modern ideas: that prenatal procedures are good, that pregnancies can be classified, imply risks, demand supervision, impose decisions, and require a large bureaucratic apparatus to arrange one's passage through the maze. What kind of woman remains after these notions are internalized?[1] In what sense is it possible to call this being a woman?

The very fact that pregnancy is intensely medicalized—its character and quality diagnosed, its progress seen in relationship to a physician—

necessarily produces an aura: the woman is led to think of disease, handicaps, intervention, cure, interruption. And, fundamentally, this is not due to the specific attitude toward abortion in the clinic to which the woman happens to come. Even a woman who is radically opposed to a termination of pregnancy and who is cared for by Catholic medical sisters in New York still submits to an interpretation of her self as being in a state that requires "scientific" management. Prenatal care programs, not an openness toward abortion, transform her body into a field of operations for technocratic and bureaucratic interventions.

And it is of course not only the pregnant woman but also the fruit of her belly that is affected by being discussed in the context of probabilities and risks which, strictly speaking, make sense only for groups; her unborn is transformed into the crumb of a population. And this is accomplished as effectively by supportive statements—the fetus is "normal"—as by the prolifers' body count of abortions, making the fetal "population" appear at a worse risk than Jews under Hitler.

It is no wonder that Maria seemed bewildered by her counselor's use of "population." I had a talk about this with my guide. Maria is the daughter of a Jibaro cane cutter who spends six weeks a year working in the sugar cane harvest near the southern coast of the island. In the old days, when coffee was still planted, he would later go up higher in the mountains to help on the plantation where his brother had a job. The mother had never ventured that far beyond her *población*. For Maria, this term has three meanings, all three still listed in most Spanish dictionaries. First, *población* means the activity of populating an area. This meaning is known to anyone familiar with the U.S. Declaration of Independence, whose author accuses the king of hampering the "population" of the colonies. Second, *población* refers to a place; it is a synonym for hamlet or village. And, third, it means the community of neighbors, of *pobladores*. Early Spanish colonial law refers to the colonists neither as subjects of the king nor, obviously, as citizens. The law governs *pobladores*. The term, as Maria knows it, is the precise opposite of a cohort of females between thirty-five and forty. *Población* is concrete, specific, unique to this valley today. It results from a purposeful activity, the cultivation of a particular piece of soil by a group of intermarried people. By contrast, a statistical population is a conglomerate of abstract characteristics. A "fetal population" reduces innumerable intimate experiences to a quantum that challenges some to engage in its management and horrifies others as a *shoah*. This leads some religious leaders to seek for sixty million aborted embryos the kind of reality the Holocaust forced on six million murdered Jews.[2]

"Mire!" "Look!" is a way of asking the woman to make her contribution to the fetal population. It is a summons to normalcy, a warning that she should worry about whether in some characteristic her insides fall outside the normal curve. The graph she is asked to look at during her visit to the clinic only serves to mystify her experience. In ways that she cannot fathom, expert professionals claim to know something about her future child, much more, in fact, than she could ever find out by herself. Long before she actually becomes a mother she is habituated to the idea that others know better and that she is dependent on being told.

4

Joanne and Susan

᠀ IN A CEREMONY honoring the achievements of Lennart Nilsson, the King of Sweden stressed the photographer's delicacy in protecting the anonymity of the women whose tissues he had made famous. Nilsson does not portray an unborn individual in a Stockholm clinic. His photography endows abstract "human life" with endearing concreteness. Fifty years after Walt Disney, I am tempted to speak of the fetus in his photographs as Bambi. Nilsson's pictures owe their power to create social reality to his skill in eliciting epistemic sentimentality—a limitless concern for the most distant stranger.

But the graphic representation of measurements brings out the inverse belief. Statistical method filters out whatever is personal. "Look! *Mire!* Your fetus is on this point of the curve, it is part of this gray column which is much smaller than the black . . . he is one of these here, not normal." And then, "I am sorry to inform you that. . . ." The counselor, like the photographer, is aware of the need for discretion: two credit hours of grief management were part of her fourth semester. Her training has provided her with learned tact. She knows how to stress the point that statistics indicate a risk, not a fact. The distinction is a kind of news that an American born to tort and damage suits might find consoling, yet Maria can only misunderstand it. In the Caribbean, where she comes from, a mite goes into the neighborhood collection every payday. That has been the custom forever. And each month a throw of the dice decides who gets the pot. It is a matter of luck, not protection against a calculated risk. The one who has been lucky pays for the monthly fiesta, sometimes more than he found in the chest. This dependence on luck has nothing to do with an awareness of probabilities. It is a celebration of secularized Providence, a joyful expression of hope among the powerless.

Perhaps the counselor's tactful explanation is just noise in Maria's ears. But if Maria gets anything out of the service the city has delivered to her, it is the news that, because of her age, her child has received a prenatal bad grade. Not the language, but the graph impresses upon her that something is wrong with her child. And the symbolic impact of such graphics on the flesh of a pregnant woman has hardly ever been studied as a health risk.

As powerful as Nilsson's photographs and slick visualization of theory might be, the symbolic impact of modern technology on the flesh reaches its climax only in clinical application. Let me take Joanne as my witness. She is a typist at a large state university where I have taught. One afternoon in the summer of 1988, she invited me to her home in a trailer park. With a few other women, I sat around an aluminum table in front of the kitchen steps of her mobile home. A postcard-size black-and-white photograph went from hand to hand. In the image, I could make out a cloudlike pattern in three or four shades of gray. To the right and left, there was a scale that went from one to sixteen. Joanne handed it to me, saying, "That's my John. His growth is normal." While she said this, her finger traced a line between one of the shadows and a mark on the scale. She rested the photo on her thick belly and told us what else was there: this dark mass the head, down there the stomach, the feet drawn up. "Look, look, that is the penis!" Weeks ago she had been told that it would be a boy. What the future mother held in her hands was a Polaroid record made during the fourth sonar examination of her belly's contents. She is divorced, her job is insecure, her parents are far away, and she did not want a second child. "However, since I know that it's human, that it belongs to me, that it moves, I could not think of an abortion." Susan, another friend, was sitting to my right. I'll never forget her response to Joanne: "What did you say? Don't you know that long before it became visible by ultrasound it was already a life?"

Of course I had read and heard about sonograms. But Joanne was the first woman who asked me to look at one showing her own insides. This wish to show me her innards was as surprising to me as the desire of my host some years before, who three times in one weekend asked me to look at a videotape of his children on the VCR. It suggested a sense of living in a world behind glass, sensually deprived on this side of the screen, overwhelmed by a collage of images I could never touch. I began to puzzle out the origins of this urge to "see" the unborn.

I find very little in mythology or folktale about this desire to see the unborn. After the advance of Ottoman armies through the Balkans and toward Vienna in the seventeenth century, a new motif appeared in European painting: turbaned soldiers slicing open the bellies of pregnant women to tear out the child. One sees that the real or imagined crime was regarded with special horror. The invisibility of the unborn seems to be protected by a widespread taboo. In the nineteenth century, however, physicians endeavored to break it. The first expression of the attempt was the stethoscope. A Doctor Laennec, the Swiss physician who for years meticulously recorded all the noises he could hear under the skin of his patients, was unable to get his ear close enough to a fat girl's heart to hear her heartbeat, so he made a roll of newspaper and, to his great surprise, the heartbeat came through clearly. By 1880, doctors carried this blason around their neck. The instrument was baptized in analogy to the micro- and telescope and named a "stethoscope," a device for *looking* into the breast. One of Laennec's pupils used this instrument on the belly of a woman in order to hear the ebbing and flowing of the amniotic sea. To his surprise, he heard 145 beats per minute through her petticoats and was proudly conscious of being the first physician to have heard a child before birth.[1]

Toward the end of the nineteenth century, X rays reached for the fetus. A woman's belly was exposed to invisible electromagnetic waves, and the shadows thrown lit up a barium-covered screen. The outlines of a tiny cranium and shortly afterward that of some tender bones were captured on the photographic plate. The six-month embryo was first seen as a tentative skeleton. In the 1930s, biomedical methods certified its presence even before the midpoint of pregnancy. In the 1940s, at the cost of a couple of guinea pigs for each test, scientific verification became even more reliable. But only in the 1960s was there a breakthrough in embryonic visualization. The embryo appeared as an echo outline of inaudible "sound." Where the tissue was more dense, it reflected the sound waves with a different intensity. These differences were measured and digitally assembled, appearing at first as a very rough black and white shadow.[2]

By the end of 1991, different shades of gray give a plastic quality to the picture, something that is still absent in 1988, when the scraggly shadow demanded the goodwill of Susan and the commentary of an expert to be "seen" as the outlines of human members. But the quality of the picture is not what is important; rather, it is the radical difference between the two women in what they name and claim to see. For Joanne, the cloudy image is that of the baby in her belly, a prenatally tested and measured son. Her friend Susan reaches "beyond" a baby in the belly. She corrects the view of the expectant mother, challenging her to grasp what is really there, calling it "a life." This difference between the photo as the prenatal shadow thrown by a baby and the photo as a medium in which "a new life" can manifest itself has hardly been examined, yet it is fundamental to the issue I want to pursue.

I sensed it when I heard the conversation in the trailer park, but it hit me with full force a few hours later when I was in the university library's rare book room facing imprints from the seventeenth and eighteenth centuries. Only in the mirror of the past could a conversation that took place two hours northwest of Three Mile Island reveal its full import. Only from that distance could I be struck by the historical newness in the perception of nature that came to the fore in this short exchange. Joanne "sees" the unborn as her baby in the digital image of a silent echo. Susan takes the electronic shadows as evidence for the presence of "a life." The facile certainty with which Joanne's eyes perceive sounds that lie below the range of her ear is as characteristic of our time as the curious logic which takes a diagnostic image—a scientific, technological "fact"—and transforms it into "evidence" that any layperson is expected to accept as sufficient to indicate the presence of a supposedly meaningful abstraction.

5

How the Body Became a Showcase

✧ CRAWLING BACK like a crab through history to the eighteenth-century Sephardic squatter, I draw triangulation points to Joanne and Susan. I attempt to place myself simultaneously in the time when the Genesis commentary was written by a Jew in Turkey *and* in the then distant 1990s trying to see Joanne's fetus and Susan's "life."

When I teach history, I traverse these centuries by showing students a route that allows them to see our "now" in the light of a "then." At each rise in the landscape I point out an image that will serve as a mnemotechnic device by which we can find our way. On the first hill I show them a popular woodcut; next, the design of a leg by Leonardo da Vinci along with two drawings he made of a woman's insides when filled; then, the drawings of fertile wombs by a learned Italian showing a fetus in the ewe and a baby in the woman; later, Hunter's atlas, a bibliographic treasure which shows the swollen womb life-size; and finally, a procession of embryos from the cabinet of curiosities kept by a prince of Kassel, Germany. I will describe these items here and reflect on these descriptions in the next chapter.

As I crawl back through history, the aluminum table in the trailer park in Pennsylvania is now far beyond the horizon—as, indeed, are the twentieth and nineteenth centuries. My immediate point of reference is the squatter, the tiny man with the open navel and closed mouth. But he is not an invention of a Jewish refugee from Spain. Hildegard von Bingen also describes him in great detail in the twelfth century:

When the woman has absorbed the seed, then, it can be formed to bring forth a human being and a little skin *(pellicula)* grows from the woman's blood, like a little container for this figure and holds it fast and encloses it . . . so that the little being lies in the middle like a person in the chamber of his house.[1]

Hildegard insists that she is speaking about a mystery that can only be suggested, not fully understood. The squatting mannequin that adorns her manuscript is an ideogram characteristic of most depictions of pregnancy during those centuries, not a picture of an anatomical entity. In its figuration it has remained as unchanged as have the letters *a* and *k* during the 1,400 years for which we have documents that show it. It conveys not the shape but the reality of the seed that grows, as if beneath the earth, in the woman. Hildegard "reveals" it to us as she reveals other realities that are hidden here below and in the heavens. The commentary of *ME'AM LO'EZ* says,

Thou shalt know that in the woman's belly the child has 248 members and . . . 365 nerves . . . as the earth has the 128 parts of a person from head to eye, from mouth to limbs . . . and with each *mishwaah*, each law that a *mensch* accomplishes, something is accomplished in the body and equally in the earth.[2]

These kinds of descriptions and miniature pictures were meant to help the contemplative mind flesh out an insight. The modern urge to provide a *fac-simile* of observations and measurements would have been totally alien. The manuscript illustration was primarily an *illuminatio*, a pictorial decoration of the text. This kind of adornment encouraged the imagination; it was not meant to be like modern illustrations, which clarify and specify the matter under discussion. It invited the reader to grasp the spiritual shape of the revelation made by Hildegard and to place it within a cosmic context. It was meant to elicit a response, not only from the eyes in the forehead but from all five inner senses, which were simply taken for granted. Its sweetness was to be tasted and smelled, its fittingness heard as a harmony. Unlike the illustration of a fact, a graphic analysis done from the writer's perspective, the iconogram of the "child" in the womb in medieval miniatures glows in its own light.

Art historians have examined the clear transition in the way light is treated in medieval and renaissance paintings. In the earlier pictures, each object is meant to be luminous, to gleam in its own light. Later, the painter takes pride in painting the light itself, which falls upon his subjects, making them visible by the rays of the sun that flood in through a window. The unborn squatter belongs to that earlier period. He shows himself to the imagination that has accepted the word of Hildegard or *ME'AM LO'EZ* about his nature.

In looking for examples of the intrauterine glow from a future child, I noticed that the shining ideogram survived well into the age of painted light. In the sixteenth, and even the eighteenth century, the human womb remains shrouded in mystery. Long after the structure of muscles and tissues has been drawn in great detail and visibly lighted by a source that comes from outside the picture's plane, only one bodily object retains the qualities of an ideogram, a glowing revelation pointing to something that cannot be seen then and there. This is the figure in the womb, which remains close to the squatter in spirit even when, in the baroque, it is drawn as a *putto*. It remains a symbol rather than a facsimile. It stands for the invisible unborn, not for its appearance. It speaks for the experience of women, not for medical knowledge about an entity or a process in the womb.

As an example of this iconographic constancy, one can examine a broadsheet by Jobst de Negker printed at Augsburg in 1538, "The Anatomy and Counterfeit of a Female Body's Inner Shaping." The woodcut is a sheet showing a woman with wide open legs sitting on a kind of barrel. The sheet folds back in the middle, and when opened, it reveals the woman's insides. Each "organ" is indicated by an ideogram: the stomach as an alchemist's vat, the liver as a five-leaved shell, the lungs as bellows, and the mother (womb), with its wings and testicles attached, as a vessel shaped like an inverted horned pear fastened to the belly by suspenders. The caption says it was shaped by God as a barrel and is connected to the female testicles by its horns. A shard from the side of the vessel has been removed, which allows me to look at the squatter inside. In this woodcut, it is a tiny person of adult proportions that presses its palms to its ears. The bellows, shell, pear, and squatter are all of a piece, elements of a well-established series of conventional images each expressing an idea rather than a word or a concrete thing.[3] Death in the guise of a skeleton man, the Trinity in the image of an eye in the center of a triangle, the tiny transparent child that glides down from God the Father's lap into the ear of the Virgin—representing the Incarnation of God's Word—all show the invisible in a similar way.

Many of the ideograms on this broadsheet can no longer be found in the learned books of the next century. The university has gotten used to autopsies by this time, and the first laborious attempts to peep into the body produce a particular kind of result. For a couple of centuries, the gory mess carved from the innards of a hanged man lying on the table at the center of the Anatomical Theater had served the learned community. It was like a screen on which they could project the traditional iconograms that arose in their minds as the professor read classical texts to explain what the barber took out of the corpse. During the seventeenth century, optical devices were created to let the new knowledge of the bowels exposed by dissection emerge. But for a long time, the principal instrument was the drawing, not the lens. On this point one man, Leonardo da Vinci, was far ahead of his time. I begin my crawl to the next hill by quoting him, because his genius foreshadowed a view that would become common sense only in our own day.

> And you who think to reveal the figure of man in words, with his limbs arranged in all their different attitudes, banish the idea from you, for the more minute your description the more you will confuse the mind of the reader and the more you will lead him away from the knowledge of the thing described. It is necessary for you to represent and describe.[4]

Leonardo here argues that the inside of the body cannot be "seen" by the naked eye, even though the anatomist has cut through its various layers. His discovery that the eye will see only what has been drawn with pen or chalk constitutes an insight not understood until much later.

Pliny the Younger, in antiquity, had already recognized the tie between illustration and text as a condition for the knowledge of nature. From all over the world he collected plants, which he pressed and attached to his descriptions. He knew that his readers would have to rely on drawings, and he also knew that in the process of copying manuscripts, drawings depart much more from the original than the text that accompanies them. He recognized the fact that, given the dependence of descriptive natural science on illustration, each generation would have to begin anew.[5]

However, Leonardo's insight on the importance of drawing as an optical device added something radically new to Pliny's understanding. Pliny deplored the fact that he could not by verbal description *transmit* knowledge gained from observing a plant. Leonardo recognized that without the optical device of drawing he could never *see* what he might later put into words. He says this very clearly in a few lines scribbled on a sheet containing a black crayon drawing. Only by drawing the various sides from above and below "can you gain true knowledge of forms, a kind of knowledge that was impossible to old and modern authors." By mere descriptions,

> the old authors could never provide true knowledge without an enormously prolix and confusing verbiage. But by choosing the shortcut of design from this and from that side, one can give full and true knowledge about these forms. For the benefit of humanity, I plead with you, my successors; I teach you the way to representation and patterning. Let not your miserly spirit stop you from printing them.[6]

I can think of no sentence which heralds more succinctly the beginning of a new epoch in the history of the gaze: the replacement of illumination by illustration. Here the ideogram yields to the facsimile, contemplative intuition of the body to analysis of its constitutive parts. Two of Leonardo's drawings of the "mother" are splendid examples of this development. In one, the vagina is cut open to reveal realistically something never seen: the penis that fills it in the act of intercourse. The other shows the fully extended pregnant womb. In the interpretation of this latter drawing, however, one point is consistently overlooked. The fully developed child that lies in that womb is not drawn from observation. It is obviously not what he would or could have seen *in situ*. With deceptive realism, Leonardo places a magnificent portrait of a *newborn* infant in the place and wrappings of an unborn. This is neither a fetus nor the drawing of an unborn.

By the eighteenth century, Leonardo's insight was commonplace. Anatomists were aware of their need for drawings when explaining the shape and functioning of the body. Illustrations were closer to the "reality" teachers wanted to describe to their students than dripping guts. In addition, since graphic techniques had improved immensely, knowledge of the *anatomical* body could be spread in a previously unsuspected way.

Another hill on our journey past horizons: In 1774, the first large

Anatomia uteri gravidi appeared. It was an atlas with thirty-four plates in folio which showed "the contents of the womb in life size with anatomical precision and artistic perfection," as the author, William Hunter, says in his introduction.

> The art of engraving supplies us, upon many occasions, with what has been the great desideratum of the lovers of science, an universal language. Nay, it conveys clearer ideas of the most natural objects than words can express, makes stronger impressions upon the mind and, to every person conversant with the subject, gives an immediate comprehension of what it represents. From the time when this art came more generally into use, it has been much more easy both to communicate and to preserve discoveries and improvements and natural knowledge has been gradually rising.[7]

The engraving of flesh and bones reveals what words could never say: "by engravings . . . the study of that art [anatomy] in which humanity is so much interested [is] both more easy and pleasant."[8]

Hunter is keenly aware of the epoch-making power of the two techniques, which now mutually support each other. He stresses the fact that the engraving opens and preserves for the eye what has been revealed and isolated in subsequent sections by the anatomist. Just as minute depictions of small details improve the engraving after successive dissections, so the engravings help the anatomist to correct *his* observations.

The body of a dead woman had fallen into Hunter's hands, and this stroke of luck provided the stuff out of which he created his authoritative atlas:

> A young woman died suddenly, when very near the end of pregnancy. The body was prepared before any sensible putrefaction had begun. The season of the year was favorable for dissection; the injection of the blood vessels proved successful; a very able painter, in this way, was found. Every part was examined in the most public manner, and the truth was thereby well authenticated.[9]

Leonardo dissected dozens of corpses, mostly those of executed criminals. He had to work at night in gruesome surroundings, and because he used no anatomical embalming, he worked under the pressure of time. Yet he continued, using the drawing as a means of investigation while comparing the detail under consideration on a number of corpses.

> In order to obtain a true and full knowledge . . . one single body was not sufficient for enough time, so that it was necessary to proceed little by little with as many bodies as would render a complete knowledge.[10]

Not so with Hunter. By this time, the public horror of dissection had declined. Injection of blood vessels with embalming fluids, which were sometimes strongly colored, had become a routine measure. And Hunter did not make the drawings with his own hand, he engaged an artist for this purpose. This one corpse supplied all the material for the standard work on the pregnant uterus. But it also did something more. Through the atlas, it helped create the idea that a pregnant woman could be placed in a category, could be made to fit an anatomical, medicalized model. The few tissues that Hunter lost he replaced by getting hold of another body and making "supplementary drawings." But with the second case, the weather was inclement, which hindered his purposes. A third body "cleared up some difficulties, and furnished some useful additional figures."

The tasks of the learned investigator and the artistic draftsman were now separated, and what would be explored and seen depended largely on the draftsman. The matter is tension-ridden. Hunter says,

> opportunities of dissecting the human pregnant uterus at leisure very rarely occur. Indeed to most anatomists, if they have happened at all, it has been but once or twice in their whole lives . . . [Therefore the anatomist] must fix on a plan, without loss of time . . . And he must keep in mind two schemes hardly compatible . . . he must dissect for his own information, in the first place, and yet conduct the inquiry so as to have good drawings made of the principal appearances; much time must be lost, and the parts must be considerably injured by long exposure to the air before the painter can actually start with his work, especially if the task be directed by an anatomist who will not allow the artist to paint from memory or imagination, but only from immediate observation.[11]

"It is well known how difficult it is to find the right kind of draftsman, *who is capable of seeing* clearly what the anatomist demands from him, and is not too stubborn to let himself be guided in this job."[12] Thus the remarks of one of Hunter's admirers, Samuel Thomas Soemmering. Four eyes and four hands bring the sight of the opened uterus onto the page, thus providing the ingredients for a potential conflict. And, in fact, one sees that the physician and the draftsman of the time are engaged in a kind of wrestling match, a competition for the appropriate visualization of the flesh. Soemmering knows that the struggle is about that which shall be seen, between the anatomist who "knows" what ought to be there and captured by the artist, and the artist who sees the object for himself:

> The attention of most draftsmen is distracted from the principal matter by details they want to represent with precision, unimportant features, such as natural shrinkages, folds caused by the exposition to the spirits used in preparation, or a compression which resulted from the conservation of the organ in a bottle. I know of more than one artist who simply cannot be weaned from accidental detail, and never learn to see only that which ought to find expression through them.[13]

With the ever more literal exploration of the body's interior the Enlightenment anatomist came to imagine it as if it were a showcase from which one object after another could be chosen and drawn. He still lived in an age when princes displayed their wealth, influence, and spirit by creating collections of freaks: the largest crystal, a two-headed lamb, bottled embryos, African masks. Scientific progress led the gaze in a new direction, into the belly, which was, however, still approached with the mind of the committed collector of new oddities. Here, nature still spoke to the physician through static images.

Twenty-five years after the publication of Hunter's atlas in London, and ten years after the outbreak of the French Revolution, Soemmering, the scholarly physician and natural scientist, published his *Icones Embryonum Humanorum* in Frankfurt-am-Main. Two large panels show the little being in twenty successive sizes and states of beauty. One sees discontinuous succession, not growth. And beauty is the criterion that guides Soemmering in his selection.

> Because beauty is, and ought to be other in embryos . . . other again in the foetus . . . in the infant . . . the child, and the adolescent, and different from beauty in the adult. Each age enjoys its

own Form and Beauty, which is much different from that which we admire in the preceding as well as the following epoch.[14]

Soemmering, an anatomist from Kassel later practicing in Frankfurt-am-Main, had taken to the latter city a large number of glass containers filled with distilled spirits of wine, in which the local prince had kept his father's collection of anatomical specimens. From this collection, he says, "I selected those archetypes that excelled by the harmony of their members, evincing the beauty corresponding to their age, and which had not yet rotted away."[15] As complex as the evolution of theoretical embryology might have been during the century that was ending—spontaneous generation had been definitely discarded—empirical embryology was still a web of assumptions and aesthetics filtered through a keen sense of transitoriness.

Soemmering did not restrict his studies to the specimens given to him by the prince. He once got hold of an "abortion"—barely the size of the smallest egg—and washed it carefully in watered wine. He tells how he opened it before the alcohol could harden its tissues and put it under the microscope. And lo, he saw a tiny creature with a head that seemed larger than the body and from this concluded that it must be *monstrosum aut corruptum*—"a wild growth or corrupted."[16]

Soemmering's *Icones* appeared in the last year of the eighteenth century. It marks a threshold. He has begun to search for an embryonic form; he reaches out toward the idea of development. But his eyes are still conditioned by tradition, which recognized only a steady increase in size. In spite of the advances of the anatomist, the embalmer, and the microscope, in spite of a new self-consciousness and independence in the draftsman, one object continues to be seen in a traditional way: the contents of the impregnated womb.

6

A Skeptical Discipline

A CORRIDOR separates the library's rare book room from my office. Crossing it, I am sometimes reminded of a childhood experience. When I would return home from vacation, the smells and colors and sounds in my room had a strange and threatening quality. After two weeks away, it was as if I saw my room for the first time, and I could not fall asleep because this most familiar place had become eerie. I experience something like this when, after some hours in the rare book room, I sit down for an interview with one of my students. The corridor separates two worlds.

When I am in the library, I am further away from the office than my eight-year-old self was from her home. Yet it is not the railway coach but the historian's discipline which establishes the distance. Because I practice as a historian, it has become second nature to me to be on both sides of the corridor, each of which demands a particular state. When I hear Joanne in the office typing the spread sheet of teaching schedules, I am in the world of ultrasound and fetus; when I am in the library, I empathize with several hundred eighteenth-century Prussian women, who consult their physician about the "stagnation of their inward flows." In the office I face Dawn, who is writing a master's thesis on family history among Irish immigrants during the potato famine, and who over the last two years has gotten into the habit of telling me about her love affairs. In a very deep sense, I am and want to be one person when I listen to her and another when I try to interpret the complaints of the Tailor's Wife, about whom I'll report in Chapter 9. Dawn uses birth control and feels responsible in doing so;

the artisan's wife and her doctor in Protestant Eisenach are beyond the pale of both fertilization and responsibility. When I am with Dawn, the Barbara over there in the rare book room occasionally shocks me; she seems to be out of her everyday mind. And she is, as every good historian has been trained to be. She has learned to see in a different context, to judge by different criteria, and to be aware of the distance between her everyday self in the office and her years-long adventure reconstructing and deciphering the significance of women's talk three hundred years ago. There is, however, something that imposes a special burden and an added discipline on the historian of the body. Crossing the corridor means more than a shift from one context to another. It means a disembodiment on one side and a reembodiment on the other. Not just the mind and the imagination, but sensual proprio-ception must shift from one epoch to another. When I cross the corridor, I ready myself for an encounter with a seventeenth-century woman; I must get hold of another self to listen to her story. Research in body history imposes on me not just a change of mind and a special sensitivity, but a readiness to experience the body in a different way and with different senses. This places the body historian in an especially difficult situation, but such a stance is necessary so that the adventure will be fruitful. On the way to the office, I am keenly aware of the transparency of modern skin.

It was Leonardo who introduced the notion that the skin can be rendered transparent. On one of his studies of the leg, a few scribbled lines state his purpose. The drawing is made with brown ink and black crayon. Only the surface of the toes and of a good part of the foot is shown. The farther one moves up the leg, the deeper are the exposed layers of tendons and muscles: Below the knee, the veins are laid bare. Above the knee, the femur becomes visible. Through this progressive revealing, Leonardo initiates the image of the transparent body that has shaped anatomical teaching well into our own time. He keeps the lower part of the leg intact and succeeds in emphasizing the elegance of the body surface by stressing its contours with light and varied hatching. This accent on the surface view guides the eye gradually into the body's depth. In one of his commentaries he notes that he draws to discover with his eyes, because otherwise he cannot see what his handiwork later reveals to him.[1] His way of drawing is prophetic. Because we are members of a tomographic generation, our way of facing the world is governed by the certainty that, as with our bodies, all reality can be penetrated by the eye, layer by layer. This is why I pointed out that my route begins with Leonardo.

If we compare this work with other anatomical drawings that appeared a few decades later, Leonardo's singularity becomes apparent. In the early sixteenth century, the University of Padua assumes leadership of a new current in anatomy. In 1543, Andreas Vesalius, then holding the chair of surgery in Padua, brought out his *De humani corporis fabrica*, the first great anatomical atlas, which contained the woodcuts of three skeleton figures and fourteen muscle figures standing in the landscape south of Padua.[2] He too uncovers the body, but his plates create an impression that is the opposite of that produced by Leonardo's leg. He shows skinned corpses of living men, each in a different attitude and with a different gesture. One imagines not an eye smoothly gliding into the depths of the body, but a skilled meat cutter violently exposing layer after layer. The result is grippingly gruesome because Vesalius's models have lost the elegance of their surface and show off their innards with self-assurance.

Among the features anatomists look for in the interior of the body, the *secreta mulierum* have a special status. Although it is true that the anatomical journey was undertaken largely in search of "female nature," the contents of the pregnant womb were the last feature the anatomist was freely able to scrutinize, as I noted in Chapter 5.

In the winter of 1592, Fabricius of Aquapendente gave a series of private lectures on the generation of animals, brutes, and man. He was a student of Fallopius, and both he and his teacher had known Vesalius. He wanted to be a follower of Aristotle and believed himself to be his only true student, since he delved into the principles of generation, picking up anatomical investigation where, according to him, Aristotle had dropped it.

It is the first beginnings of human life that I am setting before you . . . Could one tell or invent a tale more magnificent, more mysterious, or more wonderful than this? . . . for everything diligent in the whole of Nature, everything provident and elegant, God, the Father of Nature, seems to have employed in forming, nourishing, and preserving a single fetus . . . Man comes into being a tender and very fragile embryo in the confines of his mother's

womb, as if without feeling, without motion, reason or understanding, and what is more, without the use of the air and light
which we enjoy in common; and yet he is nourished, grows, and
is protected.[3]

But as an anatomist, this philosophical successor to Aristotle does
not engage in human embryology. In 1600, he issues his folio *De
formato foetu,* "On the Formed Fetus." The description of the dissection and the parts, organs, and positions of the fetus is accompanied
by thirty-three copper plates illustrating the unborn of humans and
animals. On closer inspection, however, what is shown below the peritoneum of the pregnant woman is once more, albeit larger and in more
realistic detail, the inverted horned pear we have seen in the Augsburg
broadsheet. One of the plates shows the pear cut open. The squatter
has disappeared from it, but there is no fetus either. What Fabricius
asks his draftsman to show when he finally reaches the purpose of *De
formato foetu* is an early baroque *putto.* It lies belly upward in a case,
which gives the impression of a flowerlike fountain, and gesticulates
heavenward with its arms and feet. The caption on the opposite page
informs us that this is the fetus swimming in its sweat.[4] Fabricius the
physician tried to use a knife to get at the truth. In the case of muscles
and several organs he succeeds in preparing shapes that come closer
to the way we see these things today. However, when his knife opens
the mother in the second month of pregnancy, his conception is the
same as that of Soranus of Ephesus in the second century. His knowledge about this particular part of the body is still shaped by the
metaphors that had been dominant for a millennium. I could not state
this so forthrightly if Fabricius had not engaged in something ap-
proaching comparative embryology. Besides pregnant women, pregnant animals also fell under his knife. There are sheep, calves, pigs,
dogs, sharks, and snakes. When I take his drawings of embryos from
cows, ewes, or bitches to colleagues in the department of zoology, they
are surprised to learn that Fabricius saw and represented almost the
same features they would see today. It is only in the case of the human
that the ideogram of Soranus stands as a filter between Fabricius and
the open corpse.

As another landmark on my way from the fifteenth to the twentieth
century, I want to take a late baroque etching. At this time, the scalpel
and the pen have been complemented by a large number of additional

optical devices. I call them optical because they enhance the ability to see. They are devices that improve the visibility of a decomposing corpse, which is inevitably disappearing. In addition, new methods come into use that improve the quality of illustration.

Hunter was dependent on draftsmen and etchers, but he was equally dependent on people with competencies now claimed by undertakers. Not only is the flesh lifted out of its natural darkness, but technique can overcome its tendency to decay. The art of cutting is matched by the art of preserving. The first major treatises that deal exclusively with coloring, pickling, drying, stuffing, injecting wax or liquid, and the inflating of body parts appear. And the art of engraving reaches a high point in classicist realism. The gaping body of this period occasionally conveys the impression of an open cupboard in which well-preserved organs are exposed. Whereas around 1600 Fabricius still saw an inverted pear, Hunter shows the open belly stuffed with appropriately unfolded, often mummified, organs. But the child in *utero gravido* is precisely that of Leonardo: a finished, well-delivered infant, in no way an example of a developmental stage. Hunter's team, with its anatomist, preparer, draughtsman, and etcher, has left us one of the optical instruments that shaped an epoch's perspective on the body as well as its knowledge about it. His atlas shows the woman's belly life-size. But it was expensive and could be owned only by a few. The technical breakthrough which made it possible to popularize Hunter's point of view and his vision appeared more than a generation after his atlas, in Darwin's youth. This innovation was wood engraving.

The technique of engraving wood marks the end of a story which began with the woodcut in the thirteenth century. In the woodcut, an age-old method of printing pictures on textiles, a small knife is used to cut away the wood from between the lines so that only the lines and surfaces to be printed remain on the plane of the wood. This is then inked. Only a few prints can be made from one block. Wood engraving, the new technique of the late eighteenth century, made it possible to produce a thousand prints, and they could be kept small enough to fit in a box on the printed page. They provided the first cheap technique for illustrating popular books. For innumerable people, treatises and journals illustrated by anatomical wood engravings provided the first visualization of their own body's interior.

Graphic technique improved immensely between the beginning of the nineteenth century and the 1965 issue of *Life*. And during the latter part of this period, anatomical graphics conveyed the impression of a photograph. For a good 150 years the printed and illustrated page remained the primary source for the interpretation of Everyman's body. In this mode of perception, the internal organs are conceptually and emotionally grasped as so many discrete things: from the aorta to the tear duct to the pores; from the uterus to the placenta to the umbilical cord to the fetus. This atomistic mode of perception is not affected by the dominance of successive biomedical models of physiology, which might focus more on organs, tissues, and cells, or on body chemistry. Then Darwin's students introduced a more dynamic model into Soemmering's fetal parade. Around the turn of the century, the transparent body became a display object that for didactic purposes could be disassembled and reassembled with successive developmental models of the fetus. This body came into use in the high schools. My great-aunt once told me that in the fourth month of her pregnancy she was certain she carried a little fish in her womb.

And my generation was still socialized into this atomistic view. I will never forget the wall charts that surrounded me in the classroom during one entire school year. One showed the skeleton, one the muscles, another the nerves, another the urogenital apparatus, and the last one internal secretions. I am a member of the generation that never detached its own body from these pictures. Years later, at the beginning of the women's movement, similar diagrams were stuck to the kitchen wall, and we tried to discover these internal organs within ourselves, in the mirror of a speculum. Hunter's showcase body, originally affordable to only a few libraries, which permitted the elites to acquire a bibliophile body, became a subject for grammar school examinations. In the 1960s, self-care and responsible living became fashionable slogans. In the paperback book shops, the section on health outgrew and overlapped with ecology and women's studies. Fashionable physicians joined gurus, recommending the visualization of one's interior body as a form of therapy. Skin completely ceased to be a cover whose removal had always been problematical, a clear horizon.

An epoch had come to an end. The way through this epoch led from Leonardo's intention to let the eye be directed by the drawing hand, to the skinning done by Vesalius, to the disclosures of Fabricius, to Hunter's showcase body, to Soemmering's parade of beauties preserved in spirits. At each step we had to act as skeptics, which in Greek means acting with disciplined eyes. At each stage we had to protect our gaze from conceptions which belonged to the following period. Only when we attempt to look at each of these pictures with the eyes that saw them in their own time can these drawings, woodcuts, and etchings convey the sensual experiences that correspond to their respective eras.

When I cross the corridor between the old books and the office, I do not arrive in the place where my generation grew up. Not only my schooling, but also my committed struggles as a feminist presupposed a kind of body which, for the world of Joanne and Dawn, must appear hopelessly dated. My *libido videndi* could still be satisfied by my father's post–World War I encyclopedia, in which I could peel off successive transparent pages showing body surface, nervous system, and digestive organs before I reached the reproductive apparatus in its male and female versions. And here I also became acquainted with the baby in the womb. *Apparatus* and *system*, when I first heard them, sounded like stilted synonyms for *organism* or *connection*. When I cross the corridor I move into the milieu of modern women among whom the woman I was made to be is, in subtle ways, strange. In the late 1960s, when we used the speculum, we thought we were radicals, breaking the last taboo. In fact, we were radicals only in the sense that we participated in Leonardo's project, taking just one more step. A greater step—and break—came later.

When students tell me, "I must take care of my system," or, "My system cannot take this stress," or, "I cannot survive in this system," they believe what they say. And in comparison to my struggle for my own body, what they say constitutes a radical break. I noticed this clearly in my teaching. Although I still mapped the anatomical atlas upon my own interior, for today's students Hunter's atlas and the celluloid pages in a 1920 encyclopedia are equally distant. They perceive themselves in terms of feedback within a psychophysiological system. Not only in biology and sociology, but also, increasingly, in areas such as literary studies and art history, students are taught to look for complex feedback and communication within a system. Their bodies are transistorized rather than transparent. I hear them complain about what is done to women by living "in the system" and, proud of their understanding of obscure authors, they define themselves as cyborgs, symbiotic beings resulting from an interface between the cybernetic and the organic.

7

The Public Fetus

ᴓ ON DECEMBER 6, 1987, the Secretary-General of the conservative Christian Union Party of Germany, Edmund Stoiber, requested that the words "abortion," and "termination of pregnancy" be stricken from the federal statutes and be replaced with the words "killing of human life." In 1990 Rita Suessmuth, the president of the German parliament, proposed broad legislation to protect "life." She formulated a proposed amendment to the German Constitution, art. 2, sect. 2, which reads: "The Constitution protects in a special way life that is unborn, handicapped or dying" *(das ungeborene, behinderte und sterbende Leben)*. For Rita Waschbuesch, the president of the Central Committee of German Catholics, any law which restricts the protection of life to the regulation of abortion belittles the issue. The dignity of prenatal life demands that embryos *in vitro* be given legal standing equal to that of embryos *in vivo*, because each embryo is an individual life, be it in a test tube or a womb. Other women are also formally demanding compassion for the "motherless life" in the lab. There is even a movement to redefine the subject of the German juridical system as "a life"— from womb to tomb. A colleague speaks about a trend which politicizes a strange sentimentalism aimed not at amending the Constitution but at the replacement of a Constitution for "persons" by one for "lives." Redefinitions of who is a subject of a legal system have been attempted before. One immediately thinks of the refusal by Christians and Jews to honor Caesar's image, or of the conspiracy of burghers that gave rise to the medieval city, or of the replacement of the subject by the citizen in the American and French Revolutions. But I want to argue that the replacement of a citizen by "a life" is a change of a much more radical nature.

In the understandable attempt to set limits and provide safeguards, a legal system meant to govern mutually recognizable persons is in danger of being reduced to an administrative system providing professional optimization of a biological concept—a life. The center of the German controversy is ostensibly occupied by discussions about the range within which the state should protect persons. But what all parties engaged in the debate fail to notice is that by giving legal status to "a life," something beyond the evidence available to the common man, a so-called fact of a biological character is moved to the center of the legal system. The contending parties outdo each other in their rhetorical show of "critical competence" in biology and systems analysis, while at the same time legitimating the dignity and weightiness of a pseudo-reality, "a life." Throughout the course of this discussion, which has been reported on the front pages of the newspapers for a decade now, the existence of "life" as a substantive reality has been accepted as unquestionable. One cannot help but ask, how did this happen? And why is there no controversy about the emergence of what may be a legal monstrosity?

I will deal with these questions from just one side: I want to explore when and how what women have in their bellies for nine months came to be considered "a life." I ask these questions because, in my view, a linguistic and semantic innovation resulting from the debate about abortion can deeply change what it means to be a woman. In fact, I believe that here we face an unprecedented threat of particular significance to women now entering childbearing age. Scientifically established "facts" pertaining to conception and birth are graphically publicized by the general media and thereby transformed into material for public events. Seemingly tangible reality appears in photographs or is pointed out by TV experts. But what if the facts are only modern phantoms? Then, through the interplay of imagination and media, these highly suggestive images take on final shape in the flesh of experience. They congeal into something resembling a neo-plasm, such as Joanne's fetus or Susan's "life," in the bodies experienced by pregnant women. Pregnant women today experience their bodies in a historically unprecedented way.

Feminist studies have called attention to the political significance of the public exposition of the fetus.[1] On billboards and in advertisements, the Ethiopian child with its bloated belly is replaced by a doll-like icon with a huge head. Both pictures suggest helplessness and victimhood, one appealing primarily to the purse, the other to the vote. Feminist research shows that the public proliferation of fetuses has strengthened the demand for administrative control of pregnant women and the extension of legal protection for the fetus against its mother. It is remarkable that those who strongly oppose the public display of genitalia pay for ads that shamelessly portray what lies behind them.

Haraway

Picture in NYT of fetus holding a guitar.

But the social use of the fetal icon in the corruption of welfare discourse (as seen in the discussion of who benefits from social policies affecting women) and the obfuscation of pornography (all manner of revelation of woman's interior *not* being criticized as obscene) is not directly at issue. Rather, I want to explore the bodily effects of the worldwide exposure of female privacy. The fact that these somatic effects occur has been substantiated within the last few years by a number of studies.[2] Increasingly, the public image of the fetus shapes the emotional and the bodily perception of the pregnant woman. In response, a number of women are now asking themselves how they can protect their own experience of pregnancy from the intrusion of these public fetuses.

For women who are trying to move their experience out of the shadow of this powerful image, two answers are possible: appropriate one's own fetus or reject it. An increasing array of options are available to the pregnant woman intent on doing the first. There are self-help groups in which women attempt to collaborate in the "personal construction of the image of their child" and to establish bio-philic "bonding" with the unborn. Other groups stress the need for women to screen out the male bias embodied in the publicly imaged fetus, thereby strengthening their own bio-bias in favor of the fetus as a gender-specific experience.

This is the setting from which I appeal to the experience of women in the eighteenth century in order to analyze the sociogenesis and power of the historical object that stands at the center of the debate for physicians, psychologists, jurists, feminists, and clergy. I call this object the "public" fetus to emphasize my surprise at its historical novelty. *Fetus* is a Latin word. The dictionaries indicate its breadth: it means the fruits of the earth, of trees, and of the body. In a lullaby, it is the term used to address the child in the cradle. But no German dictionary of the eighteenth or nineteenth century mentions its use with today's meaning. When the word comes into the vernacular, it appears as a technical term that sounds stilted in ordinary English. A German dictionary on the history of foreign words attributes its first use to Goethe, who speaks of "the fetus that is being kept in a cupboard in Braunschweig," requesting that it be "as quickly as possible cut up, boned and prepared, since I do not know what good such a monstrum could be if one does not anatomize it to explore its inside's make-up."[3]

After 1800, *fetus* is occasionally used in speaking of a miscarriage in domestic animals to mean that something has gone wrong and that the unborn creature is dead. Physicians then adopt the term, but theologians stay with the Greek word *embryo*. Already in 1768, which means at the time of William Hunter, Reverend Cangiamilia published the first *Embryologia sacra* in Palermo. But up until the time my mother was expecting me, using the term *fetus* made you into a social worker or a nurse. Ordinarily, a woman was pregnant with child, would beget a child, or go with child, or she would carry a burden, a birth, a fruit of the womb, as the *Oxford English Dictionary* lists the now obsolete terms of the old vernacular.

Today when I do not get my menstrual period, I wait a week, perhaps a few days more. Then I face a decision. I can cross a historically unprecedented threshold and enter the world of scientific "facts" by obtaining a kit for a urine test. Seeing the result, I conjure up a fetus, and with it the abstraction "life." Like it or not, I have become involved in the modern practice of body counts, which was invented by the American military command in Vietnam and is now utilized by religious spokesmen.

When a modern woman submits to this kind of procedure, she is forced to choose between two existential attitudes, aliveness or life: on the one hand, her aliveness, on the other, life that can be added to other lives and managed. These words refer to two modes of existence, two kinds of consciousness that are not made of the same historical stuff. In the former, she feels and experiences because aliveness is simply her condition. In the latter, a scientifically established state is imputed to her by the current experts. If the test operationally verifies a hormonal change, she can be said to carry "a life" and to begin a nine-month career as its ecosystem. That is what Susan suggests Joanne has done, and she is one of an increasing number. The management of public opinion in this respect has been more effective than many people realize. I came to see this as I listened to an observation made by the staff in a German family planning center, where abortions are performed only during the first three months of pregnancy. Since the center opened ten years ago, the staff has observed the procedure of letting the patient glance at the tray containing the product of the suction process. During the last two or three years, the reaction of women to this procedure has changed. Many now see in this bloody mass the face of a child. The ideology of "a life" in the womb has been implanted in the minds of women by spokesmen from various sides of the controversy.

In this kind of atmosphere, and because of the character of the debate, women are faced with a profound and crucial choice. But it is not on the still superficial level of deciding, in principle, for or against an abortion. The choice of which I speak deals with one's personal ratification of an imputed life. Immersed in the world of biological abstractions, a woman must decide whether to be the guardian of a public image, whether to share responsibility for its protection and development with representatives of the law. Through this choice she becomes the subject of a series of needs—for counseling, prenatal testing, diagnosis, prognosis, and management, for something called "prenatal bonding." For her, motherhood becomes the carrying out of a learned process of reproduction, baby care, and education.

If a woman does not eschew the series of powerful suggestions that stamp her as the reproducer of a life, she cannot avoid patienthood under the gynecologist, sharing with him the social responsibility for the future of the life within her, including the decision about whether to remain its uterine environment or not. Once she consents to cooperate in prenatal testing and the biotechnological care and management of her insides, she is caught in a series of unavoidable "decisions" that lead from amniocentesis to the interiorization of eugenics to the scientifically guided care of a modern infant.

But a woman can refuse to accept this state and put herself outside the framework that imposes such needs. Inevitably, she then exposes herself to a series of criticisms. Some will see her as a "primitive" who deprives herself and her infant of the benefits of modern medicine. Others will see in her the romantic who places good will, emotions, and irresponsible trust above the certainties of a modern institutionalized reality. And others will dismiss her as utopian.

When I sit in the library and close my eyes, my thoughts circle around this woman. I know that for her there is no way back to what pregnancy was. Pregnant or not, she lives in the age of the public fetus, the age in which birth has been reduced to the last stage in fetal development, in which death has become the cessation of "a life." There is no way back to the unborn below the horizon. By describing what pregnancy was like in earlier times, I am not providing her with a model to emulate. I can only invite her to share my experience: that woman's flesh, in spite of all evidence to the contrary, remains quick even in the age of the fetus. I can point out the ideas, the images, the percepts that deaden. I can outline the assumptions that turn birth into a medical act and relegate abortion, spontaneous or not, to the realm of fetal management. I might even be able to provide the elements for a map, but I certainly cannot indicate a path.

8

The Legal Status of the Not-Yet

🔊 IN AUGUST 1991, the philosopher Joseph Kockelmans addressed an elite gathering of historians of science at the University of Louvain. His thesis was that, under the present circumstances, well-done studies in the history of physics cannot possibly find a readership. Laypersons cannot follow the language in which the history of elementary particles must be written. And his colleagues in the department of physics exhaust the attention of their students with the latest facts and figures, so that any reflection on the past only confuses or distracts them. Kockelmans concludes that the history of physics is either solipsistic poetry or an activity that subverts the very procedures used in teaching physics. Now, the fetus is definitely not an elementary particle. But it is a notion as alien to whatever was formerly understood to be the contents of the pregnant womb as Planck's nuclear particles are to the atoms of Democritus or Empedocles. I hope I find it easier to argue the past nonexistence of the fetus than did the great philosopher to argue the nonexistence of physics before Newton. In my case, I can count on support from all the academic fields concerned with pregnancy.

From the historical beginnings of Western medicine, the womb has been seen as a two-handled vessel used by nature for cheese making. When it is stirred and the rennetlike seed is deposited in it, its contents, menstrual blood, curdle. Aristotle provides the classical formulation: "The action of the semen of the male in 'setting' the female's secretion in the uterus is similar to that of rennet upon milk. Rennet is milk which contains vital heat, as semen does."[1] The Book of Job witnesses to the same tradition among the Semites: "Remember Lord . . . hast Thou not poured me out like milk and curdled me like cheese?" (Job 10:10). And Solomon praises the Lord by saying: "In the womb of a mother I was molded into flesh in the time of ten months, being compacted with blood of the seed of man and the pleasure that accompanieth sleep" (Wisdom 7:2). The Koran elaborates: "He created man from finely sieved clay, then he placed him as a seed in a well-guarded place, where he clotted blood and then he formed the clotted blood into a morsel of flesh and bones . . . and made a new creature" (Koran XXXIII). And in a vision, the twelfth-century Rhineland abbess Hildegard exclaims:

> You see also on the earth people carrying milk in earthen vessels and making cheese from it; these are the people in the world, both men and women, who have in their bodies human seed, from which the various races of people are procreated. One part is thick, and from it strong cheeses are made; for that strong semen, which is useful and well matured and tempered, produces energetic people, to whom brilliant spiritual and bodily gifts are given by their great and noble ancestors, making them flourish in prudence, discretion and usefulness in their works before God and Man, and the Devil finds no place in them. And one part is thin, who from it weak cheeses are curdled; for this semen, imperfectly matured and tempered in a weak season, produces weak people, who are for the most part foolish, languid and useless in their works in the sight of God and the world, not actively seeking God. But also one part is mixed with corruption, and from it bitter cheeses are formed; for that semen is basely emitted in weakness and confusion and mixed uselessly, and it produces misshapen people, who often have bitterness, adversity and oppression of heart and are thus unable to raise their minds to higher things.[2]

Over a thousand years earlier, the physicians on the Greek island of Kos had gone further: the thorough mixing of male and female seeds results in a dough "placed into the ovenlike womb. It first creates a skin, then a crust."[3] Isidore, Bishop of Seville, writing around 630—just before Spain fell into Arab hands—speaks of the fetus in his book on etymology as *quod adhuc in utero fovetur,* "what is fostered in the womb."[4]

A parallel line of images is taken from soil. A commentary on

Aristotle written in Salerno around 1100 states that "the matrix is like a field which receives the seed that takes root there. Through the influence of natural heat and the spirit, it sprouts into its depth, pushing tiny roots and branches that feed on the matrix."[5] Three hundred years later, Leonardo draws this image so we can see how the new plant entwines itself in the underbrush of the womb.

This imagery was deeply rooted in the mind of the seventeenth-century scientists who placed the womb's contents under their lenses. When Jan Swammerdam, a Dutch researcher, first found bubbles lodged in the female testicles, he was conscious of the conflict between his preconceived notion about rennet, female seed, milklike substances, and the "egg" that presented itself to his eye. Full of admiration, he wrote, "Everything in the womb partakes of the marvellous, and as offensive as it sounds to the ear and as much as it troubles the eye, we can't help but say that women do have ovaries and like certain animals do lay eggs."[6]

For us it is not easy to fathom the commotion that was created by this redefinition of woman in analogy to a hen. The endowment of women with ovaries and the understanding of generation as something analogous to the laying and hatching of eggs made it possible to understand hominization as the result of fertilization and to posit a human form within the fertilized egg. But the old "cheesy" certainties did not disappear right away. They were relocated from the menstrual blood in the womb to the white within the egg. For a good century, cosmologically, nothing changed. I have found several *casus* that gave rise to learned discussions in the University of Halle at the time of Georg Ernst Stahl (died 1734) referring to eggs curdled by a ray of the moon.[7]

One major historical task still to be accomplished is that of situating the medical tradition about pregnancy within the literary, mythological, and popular themes of each respective period. Pregnancy has always been close to a root metaphor applied in every conceivable context. One finds the pregnancy of the womb colored or interpreted by mountains "pregnant with ore," dreams "pregnant with the future" and, more important, "pregnant" concepts. Only dreams, love, and sleep and its great brother death are as polymorphous as pregnancy and its metaphorical associations.

Pregnancy, however, is not only a theme in the history of medicine and literature. The historian of law I will call upon could speak about quickening, and how and where it became a juridical fact. The prenatal person in the womb that we talk about today stands on shaky juridical ground. Indeed, in ancient Rome damages to a woman with child were consistently assessed as higher than those to a cow with calves. Roman jurists understood the prenatal person as a legal fiction somewhat analogous to a modern foundation. In Roman law the human fetus was regarded not as a legal subject but as part of a woman's body, something with the potential to become a person. The law adopted the fiction that the unborn be deemed born only when it was in its interest to do so. For this reason, viability did not exist in Roman law. Unless the child was born and recognized by a father, the fiction was retroactively extinguished. Within this legal framework, it would be nonsensical to speak of a subject in the womb protected by law.[8]

The natural person whose integrity and freedom can be protected by a legal system appears only in modern times, and it took centuries before this kind of person was first placed within the womb. The first attempt was made by the great English jurist of the eighteenth century, William Blackstone, who was aware that this was an innovation. A legal historian would also call our attention to the fact that the extension of personal law beyond the entrance of the vagina belongs to a kind of legislation profoundly different from the medieval law that exacts compensation for damages caused to a man's household by injury to his pregnant wife or servant. It is also different from the penance imposed by the church on a woman who sinned by having an abortion, or the eighteenth-century Prussian law calling for the prosecution of unmarried women who deprived the prince of potential soldiers by their abortions. In early Christian law, abortion was treated as a sin against the holiness of marriage.

Scattered Christian opinions on abortion as homicide were gathered and incorporated into the universal legislation of the Church under Gregory IX. The circumstances under which this happened speak for themselves about the nature of the fetus in question. Gregory followed a decision by Innocent III. The case put to the latter concerned a Carthusian monk who in playful banter had accidentally caused his mistress to abort. The issue submitted to the Pope was the following: Could this Carthusian priest continue to celebrate Mass?, something forbidden to anyone who had killed, whether by intent or chance. Innocent answered that the monk had incurred "irregularity," a condition making it unlawful to say Mass, only if the fruit had been quickened at the time *(si erat vivificatus conceptus)*.[9] In the Church's regulations, then, abortion legally moved directly from being a sin against the purpose of marriage to being the crime of killing a child. Without any reference to what is now called a fetus, abortion was discussed for centuries as infanticide, that is, the killing of an infant. Murder was homicide, in this case the killing of a child, *not* a concept. The law recognized infanticide, which could take place before, during, or after birth, long before the step to feticide was taken. The Law of Charles V, the so-called Carolina Criminal Law of the sixteenth century, punished only the abortion of a "living child after it had been quickened." In Germany, the concept of feticide was first introduced only in 1871 in the legislation of the new German Reich. Up to that time penal law made a fundamental distinction between the "fruit be it alive or dead" and the elimination of a fully formed child, which alone was considered killing.[10]

New regulations covering the medical action of abortion may be of greater significance than the emergence of the fetus as a subject of homicide. The criminalization of feticide happened in lockstep with the entitlement of the physician to engage in therapeutic abortion in Germany as well as in Victorian England. In the nineteenth century, therapeutic indications begin to be listed in medical textbooks. What physicians do when they provoke an abortion is never discussed as infanticide. It is framed as the "elimination of the fetus" or the "elimination of tissue." At precisely this time, when physicians are authorized to engage in fetal removal, the act they claim as a contribution to the mother's health is construed as a crime if attempted by the woman herself. One sees that the inclusion of pregnancy in the domain of professional management goes hand in hand with the exclusion of women from its control.[11]

If we consult a historian of theology, we find that he focuses on the child's ensoulment, whereas the jurist deals with the child's viability or vitality. The historian would tell us that although there was a wide range of theories about the nature of vitality among scholastic philosophers, full ensoulment was the only critical issue in theology. For many centuries, the socially recognized specialists concerned with knowledge about women—today called gynecologists—were mainly monks, men forbidden by vow to enjoy the flesh and by church law to practice medicine. Their prime instances of women in labor remained Eve, Mary, and Elizabeth. The theologian looked for the moment of ensoulment—the moment when a new soul is made out of nothing by the Creator but also the awesome instant when original sin is transmitted from Eve's flesh to the new creature.

Christian theology is centered on the womb in which God became man—Mary's womb, where human nature was wedded to the Son of God. This is the womb of the Mother of God, the new Eve, the only one preserved from the curse attached to Eve's flesh. Until quite recently, discussion of the pregnant womb in a theological context could not take place except in light of the enfleshment of God. It is almost embarrassing, therefore, to call attention to a rather unappetizing early twentieth-century discussion about intrauterine pastoral care. All Christian denominations place great importance on baptism. In the major churches infant baptism has become the rule, and in the Roman Catholic church there is a well-established tradition imposing on everyone the duty to baptize a newly born infant in danger of death. From the end of World War II well into the 1960s, the church's new concern with the fetus was reflected in a novel set of instructions. These ruled that every Catholic nurse should sprinkle water on anything she suspected might be a spontaneous abortion. While doing this, she was to pronounce the conditional formula of baptism, saying, "If you are human, I baptize you. . . ."[12]

As a historian of the body, I must look into these developments and disputes. They deeply affect the iconography of pregnancy, which in turn reveals body perceptions. Here, I want to call attention to only some of the innumerable ways in which pregnancy has been conceived and to point out that in all of them, anything resembling the biological fetus of our time is absent. Medicine over long periods knew the embryo and speculated about it in the guise of cheese and bread. Customary law recognized the value added to a woman to whom pregnancy was imputed. Christian law pioneered rules against infanticide at the orifice of the vagina and even within the womb. Theologians speculated about ensoulment and the moment when God's mercy and full redemption could be extended to the child through baptism. If the historian looks at Joanne and Susan from the vantage point of the past, she recognizes their notions and their experience as something profoundly new. She marvels at Joanne's embodiment of a visual image, of photographic pseudo-entities that become "Johnny," more real than flesh and blood. She wonders at Susan's ability to take a sonogram as evidence of "a life."

9

The Tailor's Wife

ॐ THE BODY HISTORIAN wants to know what it felt like to be
alive 250 years ago, but only slowly does she come to hear how women
spoke about their embodiment back in the time of powdered wigs. In
the library I stumble over letters and diaries in my search for traces left
by women's bodies. Most of the remains are quite indirect, since the
words of women are reported by learned men. It is the century of the
first medical case histories written in the vernacular; there are hospital
protocols and books of physicians' advice for women. What I read is so
strange that I must struggle against disbelief before I am able to take
these women at their word. It was quite a long time before women's
speech began to go together with a body, and it is a body that fits their
doctor, their pastor's sermon, and their way of life. Now, after a decade
in their company, I have the habit of looking at the present through the
texture of their statements. To illustrate what this means to me, and to
the prehistory of the fetus, I will visit the practice of a physician in
Eisenach, a town in Thuringia (now Germany).

The man's name is Johann Storch. He was the town physician of a
provincial court residence of the local princeling and consultor to the
town hall. At the time of our visit, he was about forty-three. Twenty-
five years before he had returned from two years as a student at the
University of Jena. By now, his wife has borne him two sons and five
daughters. He was a respected citizen, and his wife was probably the
only woman whom he had been able to observe with some leisure,
such as it was, under her skirts. His trade did not put him into tactile
contact with women. He listened to their complaints and stories, and

his prescriptions and counsels were the answers they expected from him. What really went on between patient and doctor in that generation has never been studied with great care. When I first ran into Storch, I had the impression that this man was an exception. I now know that his practice, in its essential characteristics, was typical of its time and place.[1]

This small-town physician kept a diary in order to pass on his experience to his younger colleagues. As an old man he published this diary, eight huge volumes on women's ailments, others on soldiers and children. He kept an accurate record of each case, noting down what he was told, what he thought about it, and what he did. I will take one case from the over one hundred collected in the fourth volume entitled *Diseases of Women Wherein Primarily Such Mishaps As Concerns Lumps, Womb Growths or Fake Fruits are Discussed Theoretically and Practically.*[2] It tells of a bony woman, the wife of a tailor, who came to see him on April 18, 1724. The woman complains that since Christmas her "monthlies" have been stuck and that, at a certain point, she imagined herself pregnant. We must not forget that seven generations ago, pregnancy was much more common than it is today. On any given day of the year, a significant number of all women between seventeen and forty in this part of Thuringia imagined themselves pregnant, as this woman describes it. Today, only a fraction of all women in that same cohort would think of themselves as being pregnant on a given day. And the symptoms of pregnancy on which modern women base their belief are different from those of Storch's patients. One knows that she has become pregnant because a vein in her neck begins to beat, another has a certain discharge from her nose, and in still another—we are told that she is a shoe repairman's wife—the blood rises to the left side of her head each time she gets pregnant. And all of Storch's women know which signs to trust. Most of the time Storch believes them, and he quotes other signs which have been observed by his colleagues and reported in the journals he reads.

The Tailor's Wife in Storch's office continues her report: Seven days ago her monthlies returned and, so she says, quite smoothly. One notices that this woman does not come to the doctor because she bleeds. A bloody discharge during pregnancy does not trouble her, nor quite a few other women whom I have met in Storch's notebooks. Blood is neither an argument against pregnancy nor a reason to be particularly upset. Yesterday, however, the flow increased so much that she swooned, and today she noticed that something leathery also left her with the blood, whose flow did not decrease. Today, when the menses stop for four months, most women would know if they are pregnant or not. What the Tailor's Wife describes appears to us like the story of an abortion, and we would look for a fetus in her discharge. We would worry that this poor woman might be suffering shock. But the wife, whose voice comes through clearly even though the physician has translated her local dialect into high German, has unambiguously told us that she imagined herself pregnant—maybe yes, maybe no. She calls the thing which left her something leathery, or more precisely, "etwas Hautigtes," something made up of skins. I have collected the words women use when they talk about this: they speak of "blood curds," "wrong growths," "burnt-out stuff," and "singed blood." Any modern physician can use my research to apply late twentieth-century diagnosis to the women he meets through the writings of Dr. Storch. But as a historian, I want to know what they and their physician saw, defined, and judged.

The woman in the physician's office continues her story: Since that thing left her she has continued to hurt as one hurts in labor. She comes to the physician, not because she had a miscarriage, but because she is perplexed by her labor pains. And this is the perception to which the physician responds. He takes her at her word and shows this by the drug he prescribes. Consider his diary entry: "Since I suspected that there might still be a big and solid mola in her, I prescribed polycrest, Venetian borax and red coral powder to be taken every four hours." He gives her the medicine he uses whenever he wants to accelerate a birth. And he sends her to see the midwife. According to the next entry on April 19, the midwife comes to see Storch to bring him "a well-rinsed mola, as large as an egg, elongated, rounded, with little skin flaps attached to it, more or less the appearance of an afterbirth."

I cannot categorize this event by our standards. I do not know if this was a spontaneous abortion or the result of several weeks' effort on the part of the woman's mother to loosen the menstrual congestion of her daughter, or if the woman herself had used one of the strong abortifacient potions that every woman would know. I can only report how Storch views case 19 from volume 4. He places her in the same category as the many other women who occasionally bring forth not children but other kinds of fruits. After closing his narration about the bony woman, he launches into several pages of learned comments.

From his own experience and what he reads in the journals, he gathers what he knows about mooncalves and moles which, by the way, are occasionally brought forth by males through a different opening. He describes "evil growths," "untoward matter," "burnt stuff," "singed skins," "bubbly lots," "inconsistent beings," and "fleshy morsels." He usually refers to these as "useless beings," "false conceptions," stagnant lumps "that nature tries to expel from the body."

What he describes in dozens of words, always within an encounter with a concrete woman whose humoral habits he has already identified, is frankly outside my own carnal knowledge. Storch defines *abortus* "as the generic word used for whatever issues from a woman's member before her time has come. It can still be alive or a child already dead or a mola or any other congress." *Abortus* means *non-* or *frustra-ortus*, some kind of birth that deviates from the appropriate one. The Germans say, as Storch explains, "es ist der Frau unrichtig gegangen . . . sie hat umgeworfen" (she has miscarried). When it happens to animals in the stable, they use a different word. In his protocols, the physician is a witness not only to the opinions and certainties of his time, but also to its ordinary tongue. Abortion, Storch says, means that nature through certain movements that are called labor pains expels in an untimely manner what is in the mother. "In Greek they say *ambliosis*, a term used by wine makers when they prune flowering shoots to prevent a superabundance of fruiting."[3]

In Storch's view, the physician, like the gardener, lends his support to nature, and nature in Storch's sensorium is very active. Learned medicine names the activities of nature with many metaphors which, in turn, give nature its characteristically baroque face. No wonder that Storch sees nature at work in the womb, expelling what is untoward rather than aborting what should have become. The whole process of generation in Storch's writings is ambiguous. It can go wrong from the very beginning.

Thus, it is possible that the *ovulum* from its inception have a frustrating *confirmatio* or *consistentia*, or that it be badly affected *emotione ex ovario*, or have been damaged *in promotione*, and thus lost its ability to grow into an appropriate fruit, remaining an unformed and misshapen *massa* which becomes an occasion for a mola or something of that kind . . . which then can take abode within the mother, sometimes alone, sometimes in company with a real child. Such growth may be taken for a pregnancy and may depart with all the pains and travail of an ordinary birth.[4]

According to our witness conception, from carnal mingling to the moment of birth, is Janus-faced. It could be "true and real" and lead to the timely appearance of a child, or "wasted, empty and useless"—a *falsum germen* that nature must purge and, from the doctor's point of view, whatever it might be, it is a *not-yet;* it is of uncertain issue.

It makes no sense to interpret this luxuriant growth of untimely fruits that issues from an organ in need of constant purging with categories now current in bioethics, or feminist or political discourse. And yet the trip to Storch's practice is helpful. It reveals the hiatus between women then and women now. Each woman brings her own story. The physician listens and interprets it in a cosmos that is common to him and them. He prescribes powdered red coral to draw their blood because he is as worried about its stagnation as they are. He acts with nature and reenforces it when something must be expelled. And with the women he hopes for a happy issue, the child.

10

The Thought Collective and the
Construction of Reality

৯ A HUGE BALLOON containing a large-headed creature with
four stumplike limbs floats near the Washington Monument during a
rally addressed by Vice President Dan Quayle. In 1990, this sky mon-
ster evokes the same object for every American: a fetus. In barely ten
years, this disconnected figure has taken on a new symbolic character.
In the early part of the century it stood for ontogenesis and was cursed
by creationists. For little Mary, it now means the brother in her
mother's belly. When it appears on a talk show, everyone knows that it
stands for prenatal human life. When the law is at stake, it signals
human rights. For some believing Christians, it is the smallest among
the children of God and everyone's neighbor. How can one explain this
almost universal recognition for the new reality symbolized by such a
strange public object?

What is the origin of this reality? How does it gain acceptance? How
does it acquire such powerful emotional significance? I shall explore
these three questions by referring to the three steps in which the
"reality" corresponding to the image is 1) scientifically created as a
fact; 2) played up by the media; and 3) literally swallowed by women.

In order to describe the synthesis occurring in these steps, I will refer
to a set of concepts shaped by a Polish bacteriologist, Dr. Ludwik
Fleck, whose courage and uncompromising curiosity have always impressed me. He was a Jew, a physician, and the serologist in the local
hospital. He had studied bacteriology, and his writings demonstrate a
remarkable breadth of philosophical and literary culture. Working in a
clinical laboratory, he struggled with questions which only became

fashionable among historians of science some decades later. The title of his 1935 book indicates its tenor: *Genesis and Development of a Scientific Fact.*[1] It deals with the interrelationship between the clinical picture of syphilis around 1920 and the diagnostic devices—dark field microscopy and the Wassermann reaction—available at that time. Fifty years before AIDS generalized the questions, this odd man from Lvov, Poland, tried to unravel the complex correlations between a positive serum test, a clinical diagnosis, and the social status of a disease.

In one of his other papers written about the same time, Fleck tries to explain the fact that only trained bacteriologists immediately recognize the club-shaped bacillus of diphtheria under the microscope; others do not see anything. By what steps does a small group reach a shared preconception at a given moment of history, and how does the resulting science shape the gaze of those involved in it? By what procedures are the perceptions presupposed by a certain science at a specific moment embodied in the eyes of the scientist? Questions of this kind became common in the history of science only in the 1950s and 1960s. For the purpose of my present argument, I will adopt Fleck's analytic terminology rather than that of his successors because it is simple, and because Fleck, unlike those who followed him, makes a distinction that is crucial in the understanding of the public fetus.

Fleck examines a group of scientists at any one historical moment as a "thought collective." From a common perspective, they look at the results of their experiments, searching for a pattern. Fleck tries to understand how this pattern takes on reality in the eye. He looks not only at bacteriologists but also at other scientists, such as anatomists. He wrote a lively essay on the Flemish anatomist Andreas Vesalius, who had the courage

> to dispense with a completely elaborated, a hundred percent consistent, highly respected science, and consistently to build a new one from confused, unstable, changeable, intertwined masses of flesh, such as the scholars of that time would have considered it to be beneath their dignity even to touch.[2]

Then, thinking of Vesalius, Fleck recalls one of his first anatomy classes. His teacher, in the act of dissection, seemed more like a sculptor than a physician. Initiating his students into the art, the teacher seemed to be engaged in sculpting from the opened corpse the shapes of vessels and organs that corresponded to the medical thought collective of the early twentieth century. Although recognizing the importance of using the scalpel to bring out the elements featured in anatomy, Fleck also noticed that the teacher discarded all that did not matter. Reflecting on these early years, Fleck describes initiation into a scientific thought collective as a process of embodying in the eye of the student the set of shapes that are normative in that science at the time. His teacher now appeared as a successor to Vesalius, who acted in the same way, searching for beauty hidden until then beneath the skin. Vesalius had to break with his own thought collective. "He had to perform his modeling according to his own intuition, his own mystical dread of the corpse discernible in the grouping of his figures," and to see what his artist drew, working against a deeply ingrained veneration for Galen.[3]

Since Fleck's time, discussions about the concept of paradigms in the history of science and about symbolic forms of perception in the history of art have woven a weighty discourse about epoch-specific sensual perception. But there is a reason why I nonetheless stick to the precursor Fleck in choosing my terminology. He makes a distinction which is of great importance in analyzing the social construction of the fetus, something never again seen with such simplicity and straightforwardness. Fleck distinguishes two aspects in the formation of a group's gaze: on the one hand, the training of the eye and imagination by the scientific thought collective and, on the other, the contextualization of the specialist's viewpoint within the everyday perspective of his time. With great sensitivity, Fleck describes the thought style of his milieu, the mode of perception reigning around the family table and in the coffeehouse among internationally oriented Polish-Jewish professionals in a small town in the 1930s—something typical for this and only this generation. And as a practicing bacteriologist, he knew that his eyes were caught, not only in the norm imposed by the collective of the laboratory, but equally by the thought style characteristic of his everyday family life. It is this double anchorage—in the laboratory and at the table—that makes the scientist a conduit through which scientific facts become confused with cultural interpretations. As a result, scientific facts, like the fetus, have a Janus-like nature.

DNA, base sequence, and *chromosome* are names for precise formulas exchanged among the members of a thought collective; they exclude sensory experience or metaphysical belief. *Life* has nothing in common with this class of terms. It is not the name of an algorithm or a formula, nor can it be used reasonably under the exclusion of values. But today, some seem to give it a scientific, experiential, *and* transcendental character, without any awareness of its historical origins and usage.

The substantive *life* appears in the natural sciences only in the second and third decades of the nineteenth century. In political, juridical, and ideological discourse, the word acquired several distinct meanings in the 1920s. But to the best of my knowledge, it has never been used as a technical term in any natural science except in those early years of the nineteenth century. And yet, at least during the 1980s, it would be difficult to remember a discussion on the future, religion, democracy, ecology, women, or hygiene without a characteristically absurd scene: an interruption from the podium or the floor by someone stating: "I, as a biologist and a woman . . ." or, "I, as a biologist and a mother . . . must say something of technical importance about life." Occasionally, I have been surprised by the caliber of the scientist who did not blush to enter the fray in this way. How can one explain this illogical claim to competency? What is the background against which the following sentences, taken from the German bishops' 1986 declaration on "The Life of Unborn Children," can be understood?

> Modern biology has proven beyond any shade of doubt that there is no such thing as the prehuman stage of the embryo in the womb . . . This is not a theological opinion or ideology. It is emphatically a fact that from the moment of conception onward we face the presence of a unique human life. The early stages of the human embryo are in no way early stages toward the human. This insight has been for a long time the common knowledge of biologists.[4]

In the exegesis of this statement, Fleck's distinctions are useful. The first part telescopes a statement about a scientific fact into ordinary language. It could be understood as follows: the nuclear material of the zygote is homologous to the mother's nuclear material, but it has a characteristic that is not replicated in any nucleus of the mother's body. Taken in this sense, the sentence does not contradict in any way the structure of the contemporary biological thought collective, although the idea would never be that simply formulated in a technical discussion. But then, in the second sentence, a break occurs: the "fact" quoted from modern biology by an ecclesiastical authority—no prehuman stage of the embryo—is used as a premise for the conclusion that human life starts with conception. Since Aristotle, this kind of illation is called a *non sequitur.* Aristotle's scientific fact, to which the claim is attached that it is common knowledge among biologists, as recast by the bishops is an empty statement. "A life" has no place in the language of science, which is called on to legitimate the affirmation, nor does it have any traditional meaning in eighteen hundred years of theological discourse.

It is Fleck's analytic approach which seems particularly apt for exposing the collusion between the modern layman's certainties and the public relations needs of money-short science. Fleck's concepts help me to understand the contribution made by news stories, magazine articles, and TV talk shows to the categories used by scientists speaking to colleagues in a neighboring field, not just to reporters. Interdisciplinary language in academe might be more complex, but it is not less pop-scientific than language used on an evening talk show. It has generated a morass of confusion between ordinary speech and scientific communication. In fact, it has become increasingly difficult to distinguish the morass of pop-science trivialities taken seriously by the ordinary person from the kind of speech which arises from conviction, from the heart. This thought style explains but does not excuse the attempts of ecclesiastic spokesmen to give worldly credibility to a theological statement by couching it in the language of pop-genetics.

The route from Erwin Chargaff's intuition that four bases suffice to construct the genetic code to some churchmen's exegesis of this text as evidence for "a life" is a long one. Base sequences formulate the synthesis of theory and observation for the genetic engineer. For the practicing physician, the same sequence leads to a diagnosis about a unique patient, providing an anamnesis that is pregnant with personal consequences. When the same physician drags his diagnosis into a public discussion, however, it is simply false to claim that Mrs. Miller's pregnancy is at stake. What is really being discussed is the public fetus and an abstraction of Mrs. Miller as its threatening environment. Not this sentient woman, but a categorical state of pregnancy—which meanwhile has congealed into a phantom image—is being proposed for discussion. An empty phantom has become a public object, dignified by its inclusion in a juridical and ecclesiastic discourse whose scientific and commonsense relevance it belies. What a vast distance separates this creature in a balloon from the Sephardic Jewish squatter. It is not even the representation of something visible, as were Nilsson's fetal corpses in 1965. Nor is it the visualization of an algorithm or a schematic drawing to facilitate a grasp of a base sequence.

This phantom appears floating in a balloon near the Washington Monument; it is carried aloft in procession next to church banners. Imagined as an immune system, it fits into modern thought styles and seeks the protection of science . . . because it is "life." This I call a "screened," that is, a media emblem.

11

The Neo-plasm in the Entrails

↪ THERE ARE several steps by which a biological fact becomes a media image and then takes on bodily consistency as the experience of pregnant women. One can reflect on how the blastocyst comes to nest in the media and then assumes bodily reality in the womb. Here I shall sketch the route taken in the sociogenesis of the embryo, from its beginning as tissue under the microscope to its final emergence as the public fetus, a central factor in today's public discourse that resurfaces in the notion of life imagined in the heads of women.

The thing is not visible in its primary form except under the microscope, and it reveals itself there only to the carefully trained eye of the initiated seeker. Most people see nothing but slowly moving slime, which flows along like so many other slimy bubbles. The eye's lens must be calibrated for the egg search; to distinguish a fertilized from a nonfertilized ovum, it must be even more finely tuned.

I have never heard of a molecular biologist who was concerned with "a life" in a petri dish. Life appears in molecular biology only in conversation, when, for example, a laboratory director seeks support for a foundation grant from his neighbor at a celebrity dinner. The egg cell becomes a life mainly when DNA is discussed on TV. One could say that the televised film *The Silent Cry* was made to substantiate a statement. One sees a former abortionist in a white coat playing the role of a trustworthy gynecologist. Next to him on the screen is a monitor, which the doctor switches on. With a pointer, he singles out cloudlike shapes, interpreting them as the beginning of a mouth here or buttocks there. Features that histologically might be recognized as tissue or the organizational stages of cells are presented in the living room as a human being; in spite of the added commentary, it is difficult to visualize, but nevertheless it is piously swallowed as "already-a-life."

Someone using this term in a statement necessarily lands in an epistemological trap. This conclusion comes from the work of the logician Heinz von Foerster, who in the 1950s was one of the first to propose research on the epistemological status of artificial intelligence. In one of his early papers on the subject, he called attention to the risks involved in using language to interpret formulas. In the development of computers at that time—the age of UNIVAC—repeated reference was made to knowledge. Consistently, the word *knowledge* was used with two incompatible meanings: first, to designate the process of cognition and second, to designate data, information, or so-called knowledge-stock. Quite frequently, *knowledge* was used indiscriminately, first in one sense, then in the other, within the first few minutes of a conversation. Von Foerster pointed out that for a participant hearing these statements only two attitudes were logically possible: to laugh or object, which would make this ambiguity the central issue of the conversation, or simply to withdraw. According to von Foerster, anyone remaining physically present without intervening during such a conversation was caught in a semantic trap like the rest. Today, whoever participates in a conversation in which "a life" is mentioned has ventured into the same logical dead end.[1]

The media use people in white coats, people with titles certifying to their academic status, and people whose credibility is bolstered by references to the prizes they have won as mouse catchers. The linguist Uwe Pörksen of Freiburg calls these people the professional "transmission belts" of technical terms into the pool of ordinary language. When technical terms reach ordinary speech by this route, a protean linguistic entity is whipped up, what Pörksen calls "amoeba words," a modern creation with unprecedented characteristics. While a technical term in a technical context must denote with such narrow precision that the halo is minimal, these same words when pronounced by the certified expert in a media event lose practically all power to denote and acquire an unlimited power to connote. This is what has happened with such terms as *information, process, sexuality, production* and several dozen others. By appealing to some academic specialty for clarification, they stress the speaker's seriousness and importance and become unchallenged elements of everyday speech. They also meet a dozen other criteria established by Pörksen, which distinguishes them from mere slogans, from the controversial key words of Raymond Williams, and from the names of new devices, such as *transistor* or *chip*. Pörksen argues convincingly that any number of amoeba words picked at random and lined up in a string result in a sequence that finds legitimacy in the appropriate academic manual.[2]

In conversation with Pörksen, I came to the conclusion that the popularization of "life" as a heavyweight noise can be understood only as a result of the corruption of public discourse by amoeba words over the last twenty years. *Life* itself is not an amoeba word, since it does not have any application as a technical term in scientific discourse. Unlike *zygote* and *fetus*, it does not stem from the language of a disciplinary thought collective. And yet it acquires motivating and emotional power from being used by experts, not only because they use it with pathos but because they claim special competence in understanding its meaning. Therefore, the semantic trap into which the use of "a life" leads is not due primarily to its ambiguity but to its vapidity.

When Dr. Smith arrives at the lab, takes off his jacket, and puts on a white coat, he enters a thought collective. His mind works on data and his concepts are rigorously interrelated. He moves in a world of base sequences. But in the evening, sitting at the family dinner table, tieless and in shirtsleeves, he has an argument with his daughter about "a life." In paternal anger, he calls upon his special competence to define what goes on in her belly.

It would be unreasonable for the scientist father to believe that his words could change his daughter's perception. But ultrasound has already done so. Seeing a sonogram of their own belly is a normal experience for many pregnant women. And the more intensive the prenatal care provided, the greater the probability that women are affected in their own bodies by the image they have learned to see on the screen. Ultrasound imaging has come to play a symbolically predominant role in prenatal care. Its rapid spread is due to a number of factors: it produces income that stays in the doctor's office; the equipment manufacturers have made it attractive; it plays on the fantasy of patients for TV-like inside news; it promises information, certainty, and control.

The visualization of ultrasound echoes was used in World War II to locate enemy submarines. According to Winston Churchill, it was one of the key factors in the Battle of Britain. The technique spread into medical practice, where it enabled surgeons to operate in the dark. It has been used in gynecology to take tissue samples without damaging mother or child. The Federal Republic of Germany was the first nation to establish two prenatal fetal soundings as a national guideline. Yet doubts about such indiscriminate application have frequently been voiced. Prolife groups have opposed it under the assumption that it can only justify an increase in abortions. Other groups, including some prolife people, support its broad use to ensure fetal rights for corrective medical intervention. These same groups, however, are also ready with accusations of malpractice. In Germany, 70 percent of malformations are overlooked by physicians involved in the interpretation of sonograms, while 30 percent of supposed malformations later prove to be overzealous imputations. Diagnostic error has been frequent enough over a number of years to justify a current inquiry into the psychic damage it has done. Another objection comes from those who suspect that tissue damage from the weak radiation of 2 to 10MHz used in the diagnostic device will show up only after several years. But few question the risks involved in the new color Doppler-Sonography that promises a much higher diagnostic reliability.

Feminist critics have called attention to one more consequence of mass screening by sonar: it inflates the "population" deemed at risk in pregnancy. They argue that a technique developed for the benefit of women at risk is now being advocated as a test for every pregnant woman to certify the absence of pathology. Means and ends are turned topsy-turvy, while the diagnosis of untreatable cases has increased sharply. From a historical perspective, it is remarkable how fast the new device has atrophied the skill of palpation among physicians, a skill they took over from midwives barely two hundred years ago.

One must go much further, however, to make a well-rounded assessment of ultrasound obstetrics. A medical and social evaluation of the technique is only indirectly relevant to the history of the public fetus, but it was necessary to touch upon it to sketch in the background against which I can examine the somatic potential of the technique: how this technology engenders the soma or body it examines. And it is this social construction of the body's reality that I want to place in the center of my assessment of technology. What I have said about ultrasound so far explores technical side effects by asking what technique does not what technique says, even if it says it quite convincingly.

The latter is the issue I want to stress. Of course, the procedure does a lot of things it was not primarily designed to do. It multiplies diagnosis beyond therapeutic potentials, it affects tissues, it changes the juridical position of women, it creates new needs and jobs, it opens new alternatives in public health, it introduces new qualitative distinctions into pregnancies, it excludes most pregnant women from a service worldwide TV considers a necessity. However, there is another approach to the assessment of technique that is specifically relevant to the historian. This approach explores new forms of perception, images, concepts, and attitudes that have resulted from the creation and application of a particular technique. This form of technology assessment was common to all the projects pursued in conversation by the group of friends with whom this essay was written. And what does technique say, not only to those who are served by it as clients, but also to the professionals who apply it? What happens to the perception of both of these groups? Further, what does a new technique say to those it leaves out? What does all the excitement about the moon landing, heart transplants, *in vitro* fertilization, and the other acts in the professional show say to those who neither earn their living in rocket design nor get a chance at a pacemaker? As long as the Concorde flies, the Boeing 747 is a slow plane. And the glossy photo in Joanne's hands stamps all the pregnant women before her as unenlightened, blind, unrealistic, and incompetent to relate to their own fetus in a similar way.

The critical historian of technology can be interested primarily in how Americans in the mid-twentieth century came to believe that movement over the earth occurs by getting into a car, that evacuation demands running water, that "seeing" takes place mostly behind glass or plastic. She is also interested in how Joanne came to bond with her fetus, or with someone else's fetus, as with a brother. Ultrasound got into the operating room in the 1970s as a subsidiary instrument for the surgeon and then into the offices of a few gynecologists as a claim to prestige. It became essential for state-of-the-art prognosis, "user friendly" in a decisive way. The screen was so arranged that the pregnant woman could join her physician in real time to view the inside of her belly. She no longer had to rely on word of mouth or medical judgment to interiorize the emblem from the screen. With her own eyes, she could now pretend to see reality in the cloudy image derived from her insides. And in this luminescence, her exposed innards throw a shadow over the future. She takes a further step—a giant leap—toward becoming a participant in her own skinning, in the dissolution of the historical frontier between inside and outside. Her belly and the thing in the balloon on the Washington Mall fuse: her pregnancy is overshadowed by the public fetus. The abstraction of the fetus as a "new life" takes on the consistency of a neoplasm.

The historian can tell about the loss of horizon, the desire to see what is absent or what lies beyond the rainbow, the steps that led to the creation of the transparent body or the disappearance of shame. She can point these out as conditions for the state of mind in which the ectoplasm vaporously emanating from the media is turned by so many women into an experience of neoplastic life. In doing so, the historian can occasionally suggest the use of common sense or black humor. This is what one woman wrote in her diary:

> July 23rd. 9 o'clock at the university clinic. This time it is a very young doctor. He looks at the sonar screen, shakes his head a few times, clams up and leaves me there with the contact paste on my belly. At the door he says, "Strange, very strange . . ." The minutes until the chief joins him seem endless. Finally, he arrives. Expertly, he grasps the instrument, stares for a moment and says, "What do you want? That's the stomach." Hearing that, I got rid of the obsession with a fetus and decided to wait for my child.[3]

12

Quickening and the King's Mistress

ॐ ON JANUARY 1, 1663, Samuel Pepys records in his diary that the king's mistress "quickened at my Lord Gerrard's at dinner, and cried out that she was undone. And all the lords and men were fain to quit the room, and women called to help her."[1] A movement in the belly changed the status of the mistress, and she is the one who feels and publicizes it. From the moment of her testimony, the evening's mixed company accepts her pregnancy as a social fact. This was a time when women quickened; it was taken for granted that women have this experience, make it public, and thereby establish the fact of a pregnancy.

Quickening has a well-established iconography. Children in Christian families used to be told about the Angel Gabriel visiting the Virgin Mary to announce that she had been chosen by God to become the Mother of God. She consented, "May it be to me as you have said." Shortly after, she "hurried to a town in the hill country of Judea" to visit her cousin, Elizabeth. Many altarpieces show the encounter of the Virgin with Elizabeth. "When Elizabeth heard Mary's greeting, the baby leaped in her womb" (Luke 1:26–45). The child that quickened was John, known as the Precursor or the Baptist, whom Elizabeth had miraculously conceived long after her days were over. In his mother's belly, he becomes the first witness to the divinity of the child in the younger woman. There are many paintings that depict the event, the two children frequently shown within a nimbus that lights up within the folds of the two women's dresses. Mary's son, Jesus, is sometimes presented as an infant, occasionally with a crown on his head or a cross on his shoulders, while John, his cousin, already wears the prophet's camel hair garment or holds a baptismal conch shell.[2] From their earliest years, boys and girls learned that the child announces itself to its mother.

Today, consciousness of pregnancy starts in a very different way. Women are informed by mail, when the test results come from the lab, or they buy the latest "do-it-yourself" test kit and discover the circular precipitate at the bottom of the urine jar in their own bathroom. A scientific, technological test rather than a kick urges the woman to change her self-image. The lab report constitutes privileged information supposedly shielded from any third party, while the quickening of the king's mistress was a public social event. Bernard Nathanson, the American gynecologist, stresses this point: "Quickening has been eliminated by science since the 19th century, though it remains an important event emotionally for the woman patient when she feels alpha stir within her for the first time. We know that alpha actually is in motion as much as ten weeks previously."[3]

Quickening has not only been eliminated by science, it has also been dropped from English usage. According to the OED, by the middle of the nineteenth century it had already become rare in reference to the felt stirrings indicating the presence of a child, a new living creature. In my women's studies class in an American university, half of the students did not know the word at all. This rapid and radical obsolescence may be one of the reasons why women historians have not made quickening into a subject of research. During the last ten years, the monthlies, male seed, swooning pleasure, and wet dreams of former times have appeared in the titles of learned monographs, but there is no historical literature on quickening.

The disappearance of quickening is not an isolated phenomenon. The first stirring of the unborn is part of a whole set of experiences that lie outside the blinders of historiographers. Historians deal primarily with the visible remains of visible things. With great competence and some success they reconstruct the sounds of the past from visual traces: old dialects, melodies, speech forms. A very few historians have tried to reconstruct what appealed to people's taste or what the past smelled like. Significantly, its stench has aroused more interest than its aromas, but the sense of touch has hardly been pursued at all in its historical dimension. It is difficult to describe and leaves only indirect traces. No wonder that an inner touch experienced only by women has gone unobserved and unnoted. When historians have described the joys, pleasures, and ecstasies of the flesh, they have always implied that women experience something analogous. It now seems past time to focus on quickening—coming to life—even if at least half of the readers wonder.

The quickening of the king's mistress derived its decisive social power from the then acknowledged fact that women experience a bodily reality unknown to men. The lords quit the room because they recognized that what was happening was real although entirely beyond their experience or grasp. The culture of the time accepted the dissymmetric complementarity of male and female bodies. Pepys, who recorded his own dalliances, here recognizes that he is out of place. But the lords certainly do not leave out of prudery, nor do they accept the mistress's testimony out of gallantry. They are immersed in a culture in which the social status of pregnancy ultimately depended on the woman's statement about her quickening. Today, this sphere of publicly recognized and impenetrable female intimacy has been destroyed.

Step by step, the physician's finger, then his stethoscope, later X rays, tests, and sonar have invaded woman's gendered interior and opened it to nongendered public gaze. Pregnancy has become operationally verifiable. Women of my generation look at their insides with medical optics that create scientific facts. Now, quickening is at best a feeble reminder of what a woman already "knows." This characteristic experience, which leaves neither bloody nor slimy traces, has lost its former social relevance.

This is why the history of quickening is a key to a realm of the past hitherto closed to the historian: the study of perceptions that lie in the dark, inaccessible to notions, ideas, and styles of visualization. For women's history, quickening is a crucial experience that questions the current attachment of the entire field to the sensibilities of the present. Women historians are no less blinded than men by the visible body they believe they possess. Their attempts to unmask male bias, which shapes or distorts current worldviews, often disables them so that they cannot recognize bio-bias. By bio-bias I mean the uncritical subservience of the humanist to half-digested biological facts. In the history of women, this bio-bias becomes obvious when pregnancy in other epochs is construed as if it were a process leading from fertilization through nesting through fetal stages to birth—a process incompletely or imperfectly understood by the people of that time.

When I call for a history of quickening itself, I do not mean to imply that it has never been studied in historical works. Angus McLaren examines the elimination of quickening as a legal category in England. In common law, quickening was the juristic criterion for the possibility of considering the fact of abortion. William Blackstone, in his *Commentaries on the Laws of England,* states, "Life is the immediate gift of God, a right inherent by nature in each individual: and it begins in the contemplation of law as soon as an infant is able to stir in the mother's womb."[4] Only by aborting a woman "quick with child" could a felony be committed. As McLaren shows, this changes in the early nineteenth century. Physicians attacked quickening as a criterion because they wanted to challenge the court's reliance on women and jury matrons. They sought to promote themselves as medical experts.[5]

With respect to America, James Mohr notes:

> The common law did not formally recognize the existence of a fetus in criminal cases until it had quickened . . . The upshot was that American women in 1800 were legally free to attempt to terminate a condition that might turn out to have been a pregnancy until the existence of that pregnancy was incontrovertibly confirmed by the perception of fetal movement.[6]

The historian Carol Smith-Rosenberg is another witness to the same sociogenesis of "criminal abortion" in the United States. As she points out, in the period after 1860, the newly formed American Medical Association, in cooperation with the Roman Catholic and some Protestant churches, successfully lobbied to create the legal concept of criminal abortion for the first months of pregnancy. Since then, physicians acting for "nonmedical" reasons and all women who induce the abortion of a nonquickened fruit have been criminalized.[7]

13

Fluxes and Stagnations

A RETURN VISIT to the practice of Dr. Johann Storch will allow me to recover the meaning of quickening insofar as a physician's protocols in a market and garrison town in Thuringia can reveal the sensed reality of women's bodies. Such a visit furnishes the atmosphere within which we can pursue the following question: Can an inner, felt experience characteristic of women and sensed by them alone, and recognized as something alien by men, be brought back from the past by a modern historian? Is it possible to describe and interpret the events of an eighteenth-century physician's practice so that the legislator accustomed to the consumption of computer software, the voter informed by what he learns from TV, and the cleric leaning on the "facts" of biologists will listen, wonder, reflect, and take a second look at current legislative proposals? I believe it to be the task of the historian to challenge jurist and theologian, feminist and biologist. As I have learned, pregnancy was once a publicly recognized, haptic state of woman known essentially through her own testimony. This has changed radically. But when it is understood, a more general insight immediately suggests itself: during the last fifteen years a scientific abstraction has been clothed in seemingly tangible characteristics and has thus contributed decisively to making reality into a phantom.

On 15 March 1729, the wife of the quartermaster of a Hessian regiment came to see Dr. Storch. He was then thirty years old and had already begun to record his daily encounters with patients in a diary. Like most of the cases, this one also starts with a note on the woman's appearance. She is of "healthy coloring" and "good looking." Then he enters her complaint. Her monthlies ordinarily came on time and in small quantity, but for the last thirty-five weeks they have ceased. Her belly has swollen, but she has felt no stirring of a fruit. Recalling that at the time of cessation seven months earlier, she had eaten cake that was still warm from the oven and had not become sick to her stomach, and also observing that now she was occasionally tired, she wondered if, after all, she had become pregnant. "Under these dubious circumstances," Storch says, "I prescribed abundant blood-letting from the ankle," which was administered within a day. Immediately after the bleeding, the longed-for quickening of the fruit occurred. With it the Quartermaster's Wife acquired the certainty of being pregnant. Storch ends the case, like most, with a critical self-reflection. Since the woman had small menses, he could use the drastic means of blood-letting at one of her lower extremities without danger of inducing an abortion.

This protocol is of medium length. As case 115, it occupies pages 508 and 509 of volume 3 (on pregnancy) of *Diseases of Women*.[1] I have come to know these women because each is characterized in the first sentence of the entry: there is the "sulking sixteen-year-old daughter of a well-to-do burgher of angry disposition," a "lame wench with a well-established painful flow from her hip," "a fragile, sanguine and choleric, albeit full-blooded lady of twenty, married for seventeen weeks to a robust, wild and unchaste man of thirty . . . whose menses had dried up at her wedding."

Storch's anamnesis always starts out with his evaluation of the patient's social status and her humoral character. These two preambles, status and character, set the outer and inner stages for the story to which he listens. What each patient brings to Storch is not a body to be looked at or palpated but a story that has been enfleshed. This major part of anamnesis is taken in by Storch's ears, not by his eyes. Not infrequently, the woman does not even show up but sends a messenger with her story, who then fetches the prescription. Each encounter, each visit, could best be called a biology, literally the "telling of a bios," a curriculum vitae. When the patient feels impelled to visit the doctor, which might be once in her lifetime, he enters her story. And what Storch listens for is the history of her "body movements," a term which then had a much broader meaning than it does today. His treatment interacts with the narrative flow in the story he is told.

Like many of the patients, the Quartermaster's Wife begins with a report on the ordinary nature of her flows. Flows in the early eighteenth century are not limited to women. Both men and women at this time must spontaneously bleed to be well; if necessary, they are bled. In his treatise concerned with the *Diseases and Infirmities of Soldiers,* male flows draw Storch's attention. They come mostly from varicose feet, from festering wounds, or from the "golden vein" (the contemporary expression for hemorrhoidal bleeding). What distinguishes women, what genders their flows, is not so much frequency as regularity. The Quartermaster's Wife reports habitual, regular flows, a sign of good health.

Monthlies are just one of the many flows about which this physician is concerned. Some humors are watery, some phlegmatic, bloody, or digestive, but all of them flow beneath the skin. The physician's art consists in recognizing those flows which have been disoriented and gently pulling and pushing them into their regular orbits to return them to the direction that nature intended. A surprising consistency in this kinesthetic model of oriented flows ties the patients to the doctor and the doctor to the patients, and the same deep agreement between the learned healer and his varied patients can be observed in two or three other major collections of physicians' diaries in England.[2]

As a reader of cultural history, I am tempted to interpret this autopoesis of the body as part and parcel of the baroque way of life—of Bach's fugues and powdered wigs at the court of Friedrich I of Prussia. And I have no doubt that within limits, women's self-presentation to the doctor could be studied alongside the minuet and the new style of fencing, analyzed by Rudolph zur Lippe.[3] But for a body historian, this would be like putting the cart before the horse, collapsing body history into *Kulturgeschichte,* or cultural history. Body history has its own specific nuances, actors, perceptions, and inner forms. One must be attentive to these, although comparable forms of haptic dynamics in body perception are also characteristic of other times.

Body history that is carefully done reveals a surprising amplitude of possibilities, all of them in stark contrast to the kind of body we now take for granted. Several studies published during the last twenty years allow the reader to approach the otherness of past experience. Marie-Christine Pouchelle has studied the motives that shaped the writings of Henry de Mondeville, the court surgeon of Philip the Good, king of France. In his *Chirurgia,* written in 1306, the root metaphor for the body's interior is some kind of enclosure—the jewel box, the cell, the tabernacle, the reliquary, the ark—forming a microcosmos within a many-layered macrocosmos, with appropriate spheres for plants, social strata, and stars.[4] Two other historians, Carolyn Bynum and Grete Luers, have independently studied the writings of Mechthild, a nun living in Magdeburg fifty years earlier, where the basic metaphor for the body is (God's) flowing light intermingling with darker humors, which combine to nourish and clean and soothe.[5]

> And behold by means of the hidden plan of the heavenly creator, this second brightness set itself in motion . . . this means that—according to the secret and hidden order and will of God—when an infant has been conceived in its mother's womb, it will receive a spirit at the right time and will move its body. This is just like the earth when it uncovers itself and brings forth flowers and fruit after the dew and rain have fallen on it.[6]

At the height of the twelfth-century belief that the world is held in God's hand—another expression for the analogy of being—Hildegard of Bingen adds her voice. And she continues:

> As I said, what is this breath that vivifies, except the soul entering into this shape, according to the will of the Almighty, strengthening it and fortifying it so that it can be alive? It wanders throughout this creature like a caterpillar spinning its cocoon, the soul being covered and enclosed as in a house.[7]

As variegated and differently textured as the experienced bodies of the past have been, they resemble each other in one regard: their sensed shape, felt movements, and points of orientation were perceived by touch and verbally expressed by the corresponding metaphors. To be embodied meant to be engulfed in dynamics that were entirely tactile. Today's optical model reduces the importance of this way of perceiving the self. And contemporary attempts to recover body consciousness quite often do so by teaching adepts to visualize their body interior, thus embodying the pictures in an anatomical atlas.

The women who come to Storch are driven mainly by the sense that something in their inner dynamics has gone awry. They usually complain of stagnation. Their deepest fears center on the stoppage of flow and its result, an inner hardening. Clotting is the most probable cause to which they assign their ills. I am certain, however, that most of these clots are nothing which can be fathomed by magnetic resonance, ultrasound echo, or X ray. Anything can upset or disorient or congeal these flows. One woman has had a stoppage in her monthlies ever since the day her left foot slipped through the ice into a freezing brook. Another has been blocked since a piece of bad news overwhelmed her. An outbreak of anger or rage can affect the heart, "beat it down," and freeze the blood. Resentment generates stony deposits, "a kind of congery that can leave again with the urine." A flow can get stuck behind the ears or eyes, can narrow the breast or become lumps in the belly.

The women come to Dr. Storch expecting him to dissolve these stagnations. They come to be purged, to get their innards moving, to be reoriented. The physician does not use just polichrest pills or ground coral to purge their bodies of superfluous matter and entice flows back into their natural paths. Bleedings and pharmaceuticals are not the only technical means at hand for this purpose. He also uses cupping and artificially created issues in the skin. An example is the Cloth Seller in volume 8, on general diseases of the womb, who has been affected by cold drafts in the market and dampness in the cellar where she sells beer. For years she has suffered from an errant flow, which causes acute pain that wanders from her head to her side or into the thigh. Storch has an artificial wound created on her leg, a so-called fontanel, which must be kept oozing to redirect her juices. Medical history has taught us how to recognize, classify, and interpret these various therapeutic methods of past ages. But it is one thing to know the theory and technique of an age and something else to recover the felt body of that age.

The Quartermaster's Wife reports that seven months before, her monthly flow ceased. It stopped when she broke a taboo by tasting food—oven-fresh cake—that had not finished its cycle of ripening. Contrary to her expectation that she would be nauseated, amenorrhea was the only result. This now makes her question the meaning of the stoppage, especially because of her occasional tiredness and rounding belly. Storch reflects upon her uncertainty but does not touch her. He almost never touches a patient. For him, pregnancy remains doubtful as long as quickening has not become part of the story.

Dr. Storch intervenes in the life story of the Quartermaster's Wife by inducing a directional flow which animates the fruit. Immediately his patient is "quick with child." Her anguish about a false pregnancy or a "wrong growth," and the physician's doubts, are all resolved. Drawing an abundant amount of blood from the ankle, from the saphena—the "mother vein"—on the inside of the foot, was known as a drastic measure. He could well have used another of the *pellentes* or purgatives that are given. "If a woman suspects pregnancy," the well-known medical manual by Gabelkover says in 1680, "but does not have true knowledge . . . if she is with child, it will strengthen the fruit; if not, it [the *pellentes*] will purge the untoward growth."[8] In this case, venesection did provoke quickening. It could have provoked a "purging of the womb" in a woman of different constitution.

14

Hapsis and Opsis

꙲ TWO DOCUMENTS lie before me: on the left, the report of the Quartermaster's Wife, and on the right the laser printout of the preceding chapter, with passages copied from Storch that must be checked. Both are tangible things, both speak to my senses, but it would be difficult to find two objects with more sharply contrasting sensual qualities. The octavo volume printed on rag paper emanates a different aura than the thirty-two-pound bond. Reading the printout, I am satisfied that the passages I have compared are identical. But visually, the difference is jarring. Every *m* printed by the Hewlett-Packard printer is of one series, indistinguishable from any other, down to microns. This is not true of the leather-bound volumes printed in Gotha in 1751: rarely do all three feet of the letter *m* stand on the same ideal line. Though the text on my right might be identical to that on my left, the *corpus,* the body, the physical object, could not be more different. They exude different epochs.

When I have to comment on the text from the original, set in fraktur—old German type—I have made it a habit to let my eyes move to the laser transcription. This exercise forces my attention to dwell on the difference in the connotation, then and now, of every word. I need to do this exercise because the better I come to know Storch's individual female patients, the more my detachment is threatened, mainly by pity and envy. Pity for Storch's huge flock comes naturally when one reads of the sores on their feet and the lice on their skin. But the dead women get nothing from my pity, and it actually pushes us apart; romantic pining is just as divisive. It would be self-delusion to envy them their womanly strength. Embarrassment about my penicillin, which spares me their sores, cripples my ability to get their discomfort into focus. Each time I reread one of these stories, I attune myself to those concepts which might enable me to describe the distance between their "flows" and "stagnations" and my way of visualizing my ills.

Over time, woman and body do not remain the same. Distance that at first seemed expressible in years increasingly becomes something sensual and qualitative. Certainties lose their categorical closure and give way to what Rodney Needham calls "polithetic concepts." What he means by this is best expressed in a simile: A polithetic concept is like a rope. What gives strength to a hemp rope are the innumerable single fibers from which it has been twisted. If one cuts through the rope at a sufficient distance from one end, not one of the threads that contributes its strength to the rope at the beginning of the segment can be found. The rope remains a rope, but each single thread runs through for only a short distance.[1]

Something analogous happens when I follow the female body into its historical past. After only a short while, the threads I finger are no longer those I recognize within myself. I delude myself if I try to make my own flesh resonate to the words from Storch's case histories. The body I take to my doctor contains no empirical equivalent to the body Storch's patients present to him. There is nothing in me that I have been trained to equate with the rumblings and threatening stagnations his patients experience. Some authors, like Marie-Christine Pouchelle and Judith van Herik, have sought, and perhaps found, something similar in the dreams, nightmares, and analysts' records of modern women. They are capable of experiencing alternate realities and they know it.[2]

Storch's women complain about everyday happenings, and they do it with sufficient detail to enable a modern doctor to diagnose what they "really" have. But if I want to sympathize with these inner "movements," "burdens," and "uplifts," I cannot be satisfied with a translation of their complaints into the language of an internist. To diagnose a gnawing heart polyp, a term listed by the OED for the seventeenth century, as a cardial dysfunction is to miss the experience of that woman. And a sequence of "stormy seasons" raging through the breast will only be misread if it is cast into the language of Freud or Jung. Insofar as it is possible, we have to grasp the blockage of the Quartermaster's Wife as it was felt by her. And in each of my attempts to do this, I become more conscious of the cleavage between her and me as a modern historian.

Modern historians have dealt with this hiatus in different ways. Historians of science have popularized the idea of a change in paradigms. Cultural historians look to anthropology and speak about acculturation. Historians of ideas speak about epistemological breaks, rifts, or fault lines when they refer to shifts in set patterns. The history of art records changes in basic styles. Some have derived the notion of singularity from statistics, others Thom's catastrophe from systems analysis. For different purposes, these various terms designating discontinuities can be used in body history to clarify the transition from the experience of Vesalius to Hunter to Daguerre, Roentgen, or Nilsson. But all of these terms have one thing in common. They were created to describe a pattern of ideas or representations, not sensual experience. And what I am exploring about pregnancy refers to sensual experience. There is no doubt that paradigmatic change in medicine has been decisive in distinguishing different stages of embryology. But for one who is concerned with the perceived body of the woman, changes in embryology are secondary. The perception of the state of pregnancy, which is my focus, is a transition from hapsis to opsis, from the haptical to the optical hexis of the pregnant woman.

I am purposely introducing two terms which are well defined but have not entered general usage. *Hexis* is the Greek word for attitude, for the habitual state in which a person finds herself. *Hapsis* is a technical term used by psychologists to refer to perception through the sense of touch. In the 1960s, some tried to coin an equivalent English word, *sensitivity*, to describe such perceptions. I speak of haptic hexis with the intent of coining a term that describes a way of being, feeling, and sitting within oneself that is oriented not primarily by visual reference but by touch, taste, the sense of space, the feel for atmosphere.

The Greek word *opsis* simply means vision. I speak of an optical hexis when the "state" of a person is oriented primarily by visual representation, imagination, or graphics. Optical hexis has a history. Its intensity in a given epoch is strongly dependent on the cultural prevalence of optical devices. Perhaps the most influential and transforming optical device has been script, which makes ideas, concepts, or words into something that can be sensually, visibly grasped. Optical hexis is shaped by pictorial techniques. Pictures not only show but interpret one's body.

The formation of the fetus is to a large extent the history of its visualization. And, in a crucial way, a succession of new optical devices supported and defined the steps toward a greater emphasis on visualization. Leonardo explicitly conceived his drawings as optical instruments leading to carnal knowledge of a visual kind. Leeuwenhoek's lenses, Fabricius of Aquapendente's scalpel, and Hunter's choice of graphic artists mark this progression. The technogenesis of the fetal image and of embryology can be related to these instruments of visualization.

It would be a mistake, however, to limit the significance of new optical techniques to progress in speculative and applied science. The optical techniques that spread during a particular period sooner or later also shape the epoch's characteristic optical hexis. Joanne not only "saw" John on the screen, she has a facsimile of "screen-cum-John" in her purse. She identifies John with his shadow. The screen is so much a part of her hexis, her state of mind, her everyday experience, her certainties, that she never asks if fetal John would exist for her without it. She lives with most of her world behind glass and takes for granted, for real, what is shown on the screen.

During the last few years, the relationship between technique and today's epoch-specific hexis has generated an important literature. But the same cannot be said for the history of hapsis. For this neglect of the senses, except for seeing and hearing, one can immediately provide an excuse: descriptions of what is seen use clear, straightforward, colorful words; sounds can be recorded in letters or notes. But for haptic experience it is not so easy. By its very nature it is almost dumb and blind, and the vocabulary that was once available to give it expression has shrunk to a vanishing point in modern languages. It also appears that haptic experience dwindles as we come closer to the present.[3]

In the encounters between Dr. Storch and his women patients, it is obvious that in this respect they understand each other. Storch immediately grasps the haptic sense of their statements, something the historian comes to appreciate only by repeated rereading. What the women say is mostly kinesthetic: they report the experience of oriented movement. They tell him what rises and what falls, what accelerates and what gets stuck, what rushes and what has become lazy. The blood seeks outlets or it congeals on the inside. The haptic experience they report is characterized by quality and direction. It always has what the

Latin medical language of the time called a *tonus,* something like a density, a color, or a taste. Dark, thick, heavy blood disturbs and even frightens them. The dumb, weak, helpless seed of their husbands is unfit to move them. Heat overwhelms and must be sweated out. And the experiences also have an oriented intensity; they could be plotted on a vector. A mathematician has told me that I am describing the body as a tensor: a set of vectors with different orientations and intensities. The kinesthetic body of these women involves a complex experience of orientation. They come to the doctor to reorient themselves. As far as I can grasp it, pregnancy represents a special instance in this haptic hexis, a reorientation in the kinesthetic state of the Tailor's Wife, the Cloth Seller, the Quartermaster's Wife. The experience of quickening happens when something in them orients itself, manifesting its own aliveness. Until recently, the woman's own witness to this particularly moment in her haptic hexis was the only way to know she was pregnant.

15

The Uterine Police

ONCE THERE WAS a time when pregnant women quickened, and when this happened they knew they were with child. It might take place in the drawing room, as we know from the king's mistress, but most of the time it occurred while hoeing, cooking, or sewing. Making this known, the woman's declaration changed her state. A modern woman has no comparable power to redefine her social status by making a statement about her body. In our society, we are accepted as sick, healthy, or pregnant only when we are certified as such by a professional. Yet from our perspective, we think the women of 1720 were at the mercy of their bodies. They had nothing like our access to a lab or a clinic. What they did have was the power to testify to an experience which was not just private but intimately nonshareable, and this definitively changed their social standing. A woman might be under suspicion of pregnancy, or have been pregnant in hindsight, but without her own witness, no woman was definitely pregnant. For at least two thousand years, the annunciation of quickening took place in her own secret parts.

Susanna Margaretha Brandt, age twenty-two, a servant in Frankfurt, appeared in court in 1770 accused of having killed her newborn infant. She testified that "due to intense anger her monthly purges had stopped and thickened her belly." But until quickening, it was impossible for her to be certain of anything. And even when, later on, her belly was rumbling, neither she nor the physician could exclude the possibility that this might be due to a mole or bad gas. If her period returned, whether by nature or medicine, it could be understood by her and by her neighbors as the expected cleansing. In Margaretha's case, "a child rushed out while she was standing." In another case of alleged infanticide, "the pangs came on at night, she was alone while the child came . . . until also the rest [afterbirth] came out." The judge knew that the accused could not easily be indicted for murder. Apollonia, a maid in Nuremberg also accused of murder, insists in front of the court in 1598 that "for eight days she had felt no life and had come to the conclusion that it was rotting in her."[1]

The historian of quickening can look at these events from two sides, as a body percept or as a social perception. I did the former in my commentary on Dr. Storch, trying to interpret the transformation of a synesthetic-haptic percept of that time to a visual, self-ascribed concept today. Now I want to examine the changes in the social significance of quickening by commenting on another text. I can thus complement my reflections about the social shaping of a woman's body with remarks on the shaping of society through a symbolism implicit in body perception. And it was particularly woman's body that was used to form and interpret a new type of society. I understand the demise in the social status of quickening as an event that brings an important paradox to the surface: in the course of the nineteenth century, female innards and interiority become medically, administratively, and judicially public while, at the same time, the female exterior is privatized ideologically and culturally. These opposed but linked tendencies are both characteristic moments in the social construction of "woman" as a scientific fact, as well as in the creation of the citizen in industrial society.

On the one hand, the newly discovered "naturalness" of domesticity and motherhood, domestic work and familial sociability, the need for protection and marital dependency place women in the "private realm" in law, education, and ethics. But at the same time, science discovers and professionals control and mediate her womb as a public space. Her flesh becomes the forum whose proceedings are of immediate interest to the state and society, to public health and the church, and also to her husband. The history of quickening is like a convex mirror in which one can see this progressive, paradoxical socialization of woman. Her actual body experience becomes her own private affair, while the scientific fact that a fertilized egg has unleashed a hormonal reaction assumes a momentous social function.

Wilhelm Gottfried von Ploucquet (1744–1814) was a medico-legal expert, a physician in Tübingen, and the author of a treatise on medical ethics. He writes at just the time when quickening as a social experience is undergoing its decisive transmogrification. Ploucquet wants to transform quickening into an event that can be witnessed by the physician. The second book in his *Treatise on Violent Ways of Dying* (1788) deals with infanticide: "The movements of the fruit, inasmuch as they can be felt by an outsider or when they can be seen from the outside and are visible to the examiner, are one of the most privileged signs of pregnancy."[2]

Ploucquet sees the physician's task as "discovering pregnancies." According to him, the simplest way to achieve this end would be "the general installation of monthly public baths which should be made obligatory for each unmarried woman who is over fourteen and under forty-eight years of age." Ploucquet deemed this inspection through public bathing "the only real method" for discovering pregnancies, much more efficient than palpation to "detect the fruit from the outside." But since the establishment of such baths is not within his power, he looks for other means.[3]

Ploucquet wants to feel or see what no man has ever before attempted to feel or see, the movement of the fruit. He wants ultimately to bypass society's dependence on the testimony of women. We have become so accustomed to pregnancy tests that we need to stop for a moment to realize Ploucquet's daring. He belongs to the first generation of physicians who in the early nineteenth century palpate a woman's body. As far as he reports, however, he touches only the bellies of women who are suspected of being pregnant out of wedlock. And they are usually poor. Ploucquet and his colleagues find material for their examinations and literally pay for it with soup and a warm room, pocket money and swaddling clothes. In Strasbourg, Göttingen, Berlin, Kassel, and Munich, the inmates of maternity houses must submit to internal examination.

Ploucquet describes a series of medical interventions on the bodies of women that have become, in a more sophisticated and technically mediated way, characteristic of gynecology. He sees women "after the removal of their clothes." First the physician looks. If the initial glance gives no results, an "examination of the belly cannot be avoided." Nothing similar happened in Storch's practice barely fifty years earlier. But Ploucquet is not satisfied with looking or with a palpation of the abdomen. He might dare to move on and do an internal examination:

"This is how 'the mother' shall be examined: Have the pregnant woman stand in front of the physician who is sitting, place one or two fingers in the vagina and feel to the cervix and the *os uteri*, and thus you will find out about its state."[4]

At first sight, the gestures of vaginal exploration that have become routine could lead one to believe that Ploucquet's idea of the body's interior is comparable to that of the late nineteenth and twentieth centuries. But this would be historical nonsense. Although his procedures represent an innovation, he does not attribute a new kind of significance to the outcome of palpation. Ploucquet places the results of palpation in the same category of indicator as the other "changes outside of the mother." In doing so, he continues a tradition that has been recorded since the time of Hippocrates. Ploucquet, too, observes the eyes of the women whom he suspects of being pregnant to see if they are swollen, turbid, surrounded by blue rings, or covered by soft and hanging lids. He knows all the old signs. The humors of the pregnant rush toward the head and cause discolorations, heat blisters, abundant salivation, headaches, and reddening of the face. Every one of these signs and all of them together are for Ploucquet, as for all the doctors that preceded him, possible but uncertain indications of a pregnancy. As a doctor who faces the court, Ploucquet knows that a report about pregnancy—before birth!—is about something invisible, more or less a conjecture. He knows what had been within only when the fruit has appeared. As he notes, "Not everything which comes from the birth parts of a woman is a human being."[5]

Ploucquet studied anatomy, so he knows what there can be within the mother. But his mode of perception is such that he does not and cannot imagine successive developmental *stages* of the fruit within a living body. He wants to provide the Prussian authorities with information about a secret formation, but within the milieu in which he lives and practices, the existence of invisibles is still taken for granted. In this mentality only hearsay, learned tradition, and conjecture are possible for that which happens below the horizon; that kind of occurrence follows no set norm. The nine months of tradition are an epoch, a duration, not the length of a process. He still believes the testimony of widows who bear their husband's children ten or more months after his death. The humoral constitution of the womb, the quality of the man's embrace, and the character of the unborn taken together still influence the time it takes to hatch it.

If an infant dies, Ploucquet wants to know if it was killed, but he has no medical test to use in making a judgment. He cannot decide for murder, "since death that results from the denial of care can generally not be distinguished by decisive signs from natural death and, further, since one never knows if death has been caused by uncertainty, neglect or intent, it will be difficult ever to make a judgment."[6] How should one know if the child was left to gag on its saliva, if its hands and feet were put in cold water, or if it was accidentally smothered by its mother?

16

Synthetic Life

ॐ THE HISTORY of ideological gynecology has now led us to the epoch of fetal dominance. Its visible appearance has colonized discourse, vision, and, I would argue, the experience of the potentially or actually pregnant woman. Surreptitiously, a new ideogram, demanding a new set of attitudes, has emerged and become universally accepted. This is "life." The technotropic sentimentality with which Joanne peered through the viewer at her little John is part of a mentality now outdated. Susan clearly represents the ideal of a new type. While Joanne fleshes out the shadow and brings it closer by calling it "John," Susan quite logically distances it through disincarnation, calling it "a life."

I saw Joanne refuse a second cup of coffee out of consideration for John, to whose presence she had accommodated herself. For Susan, Joanne's reproductive state is primarily a concrete occasion to stand up for the defense of the most emotionally distant of strangers, an abstraction shorn of the pathos of the Ethiopian girl with a bloated belly or of the intrauterine thumbsucker. This shift from Joanne's to Susan's type of consciousness reflects a more general trend in the discourse of politics, medicine, ethics, and comics. Increasingly, the fetus—or even the cockroach—threatened by extinction, is used as a mere instance, a newshook, or an emblem to make a much more general statement about endangered life.

While the whale, the rain forest, the terminal Alzheimer's patient, the spina bifida infant, the botched suicide, and those affected by Karposi's sarcoma constantly emerge from a mixed bag of threatened lives, life itself finds its principal visual expression in two complementary disks:

on the one hand, the Blue Planet, on the other, the transparent pink zygote. This pair has moved to the top of the list of cult objects in the 1990s.

I have traced the history of the public fetus, from its conception as the laboratory's bastard and its legitimation and popularization by the media to its neoplastic invasion of woman's flesh. In the hope of suggesting an agenda for reflection, I have reported on breaks in bodily hexis that are typical for successive generations. At various times in this narrative I have invited the reader to flesh out for herself some old and disorienting text. In each of these instances, the effort to interpret the past in terms of its own body experience has given me the opportunity to wonder about contemporary certainties, to recognize their historical nature and, therefore, their transience before new experience yet to come.

When "life" rather than the fetus becomes the issue, however, this historical method of distancing ourselves from the present through the embodiment of the past can no longer be used. I have reached the end of a narrative thread. While I could speak about the fetus in terms of a break in body experience, of a new paradigm, of a singular turn in the story, of the transformation of hemp rope into nylon cable, this is no longer possible when my task is to discuss the replacement of the Sephardic squatter with impressions attached to a pink disk. In this recent shift from the fetus to "a life," flesh is extinguished and replaced by a disincarnate notion. According to traditional understanding, to call this a transfiguration of the flesh would be blasphemy. The "life" that dominates the current discourse of legislators, ethicists, and concerned citizens—life for which responsibility can be accepted—is diametrically opposed to that which appears in the Gospels. Its story belongs to the history of delusions, ideologies, and religions, not to the history of the body, not to the account of the Incarnation.[1]

"A life" is first of all a grammatical subject, but it is also used hypostatically as a noun referring to subjectivity in the order of reality. What is designated by the word are stages of chromosomal organization, coded genetic information, or the morphology of tissues whose existence can be verified only under laboratory conditions. Referring to these terms, legitimate only for professional observers, as "a life," one gives them a status that transcends the parameters within which the observation can be verified. When lawmakers assume a mandate to protect life, they legislate a fact that cannot be testified to by the witness of the ordinary person. The common law tradition in English-speaking countries may be one reason why in the United States the replacement of "a citizen" by "a life" has not reached the extremes found in the German Bundestag. The First Amendment protects the abuse of "life" by prolifers who, by the simple power of the term, imply murderous intent among those who do not march in their ranks. But until now, lawmakers steered clear of life. In modern Germany, the old marriage between Napoleonic Code law and Prussian administrative ordinances appears in a new dress, cut from the cloth of the U.S. Constitution by American military lawyers. The possibility that "a life" will also slip into German law cannot be excluded.

Similarly, the use of "a life" by church authorities is surprising. The Church derives its special claim to wisdom from the fact that it is the guardian of Divine Revelation, neither ordinary common sense nor scientific truth. As such, it is concerned with the administration of baptism to its children. But now it assumes responsibility for the mere existence of developmental stages of human chromosomes.

Equally surprising is the ease with which the medical profession worldwide has recently redefined its purpose. In Western tradition this had been the soothing of pain, the support of suffering, and the healing of disease. Toward the end of the nineteenth century, the physician's struggle against death shifted professional consciousness toward a new goal, but the physician was still in charge of a patient. Along with the recent discourse about life, however, this has also changed. It is no longer patients from birth to the hour of death but lives from sperm to worm that are the "subjects" of medical care. In tune with this, the German Bishops' Conference has published a declaration in which God is promoted to a "friend of life," and in which they call for legislation that would protect the deceased against the removal of their organs, "until their lives have been declared dead."[2]

I am not aware of any protest against the absurdity of this statement, which appears in three successive editions of the pamphlet. The novelty of such expressions is perhaps less surprising than the blindness to their non-sense. Not only in editorials but also in learned journals, "life" is mentioned as if it had always been around as a subject of discussion. The texts give the impression that science has always searched for the beginning of life, that medicine has always protected the life of patients, that the Church has always equated human existence with life, that the lawgiver has always considered unborn life rather than precious sons, valuable recruits, useful serfs, and legitimate heirs.

The lack of criticism about the use of "life" calls for explanation, and one lies within the competence of historians. The substantive use of the notion life in Western society has unacknowledged Christian roots. Its semantic field barely coincides with the Hindu and Buddhist cognates and constitutes a specific development beyond the Hebrew and Koranic usages of the corresponding expressions. In its strong sense as a noun, the word has taken shape from a scene in the Gospel of St. John, in which Jesus speaks to Martha, the sister of that Lazarus who, later on the same day, was quickened from the dead. Jesus says, "I am . . . life" (John 11:25). In most of the New Testament and in two thousand years of ecclesiastical usage, to "have life" means to participate as a believing Christian in the life of Christ, a mode of living which is placed in stark contrast to mere human existence. Even the dead live in Christ, and only those who live in Christ have life in this world. Of those who exist outside this relationship, the Church has consistently spoken as those who "live" under conditions of death. In this sense and only in this sense is life holy and can one speak of the sacredness of life. This is simply the traditional understanding and teaching. As Dirk von Boetticher, a German colleague, has shown, this Christian coinage has shaped the semantic field of *vita* in such a decisive way that it cannot be compared with the word field in antiquity—or, for that matter, in oriental or other languages either.[3]

Antiquity has no concept or term for substantive life. *Bios* means destiny, curriculum vitae. *Zoe* expresses the vitality and splendor of ensouled beings. *Psyche* can be used to translate the Hebrew word for blood and, occasionally, the soul. Amateur antiquarians who replace "life" in the modern context with one of these words make fools of themselves. At the same time, the modern term has none of the majesty and glory of the Old Testament *ruah*, the blowing and weaving spirit of the Almighty, which gives us an inkling of what his Son in the flesh meant when he said, "I am life."

Of course, this does not mean that the distinction between things alive and things dead, things that crawl and things that only stay put and feed was not central to premodern thought. The absence of substantive life only stresses the embodiment of aliveness, somewhat as the present discussion on substantive life reveals the disembodiment of contemporary discourse. Aristotle knows no blackness, but he knows black things; he knows no life, but he left us brilliant treatises on beings that are alive in several degrees of intensity—plants, animals, and humans who, in addition to growing and moving are endowed with speech and especially with laughter. Life as a substantive notion appears a good century after the final demotion of Aristotle as the great science teacher, or about two thousand years after his death. In 1801 Jean-Baptiste Lamarck introduced the term *biology* into the French language. The new science defined "life" as its object. Lamarck took a critical stance toward baroque botany and zoology, which had ossified as classificatory enterprises, reducing their science to the classification of new entities and scientific discussion to their reclassification. In Germany, K. F. Burdach simultaneously introduced the term *biology,* defining it as an attempt to study man from the combined perspectives of morphology, physiology, and psychology. Lamarck, like Treviranus, felt that by coining "biology," he would identify a new field of study rather than just give a name to an old one. The new biology was concerned with the functioning of living things. By focusing on the unifying entity, life, Lamarck undermined the millennial tradition that distinguished the distinct ensoulment of plants, animals, and rational man, abolishing the firmly rooted tripartition of nature. His action also relegated to irrelevance the then widespread doctrine of a successive ensoulment of the human fruit by the vegetal, animal, and, finally, spiritual-rational principle. Lamarck postulated the existence of life. Through its possession, alive beings are distinct from inorganic matter not because of their different structure but as a result of their organization. With Lamarck, the evolution of biology begins, successively searching for the genesis of this organization in tissues, then cells, then protoplasm, then the genetic code, and by now—with Rupert Sheldrake and others—in morphogenetic fields.

For the academies flourishing during the first decades of the nineteenth century, "life" was a welcome postulate for overcoming the division of their members among mechanists, vitalists, and materialists. However, life served such an ecumenical purpose for only a short moment. The shift of scientific interest toward morphology and physiology dimmed interest in life. The disappearance of life from recognized science, however, did not throw the term into oblivion. The question, "What is life?" became an appealing rhetorical slogan in the popular sciences toward the middle of the nineteenth century. Particularly in Christian apologetics, it was thrashed out in hundreds of pamphlets and books in an attempt to answer the challenge of agnostic rationalism.

By this route the word became a polymorph, full of connotations but impotent for denotation. The word has become a jack-of-all trades with disparate, almost random usages. During the 1980s, the use of the term qualified the speaker as serious, concerned, and humane. Lovelock's tautology gave it dignity: "Life is that function which optimizes the conditions for its existence."[4] While Hitler's concept of valueless life *(lebensunwertes Leben)* has come to be seen as a legal perversion, dozens of lawyers have earned their fee by representing persons who sue a gynecologist for a "wrongful life," that to which they are condemned because his "malpractice" prevented their abortion. One only has to be vaguely alert when leafing through glossy mass circulation magazines to recognize how attractive life has become for the advertising industry, how clubs, shoes, towels, toothbrushes, and travel are identified with the quality of "life."

In spite of the demeaning corruption, pretentious mystification, and aggressive waving of this empty word, almost no one, except for a few people like Daniel Worster and Wolfgang Sachs, has yet called for a historical epistemology of ecology.[5] Perhaps a reason can be surmised. Any criticism is immediately answered by someone who connects life with right or value or sacredness and, by so doing, evokes six million Jews, or sixty million fetuses, or large numbers of Kurds and Cambodians, or even the rain forests, bugs, and grasses. The four-letter word is meaningless and loaded; it can barely be analyzed, yet it is a declaration of war.

But there is another, much deeper reason that has made it difficult to analyze this maniacal brandishing of life. Life has gained prominence as nature has died. The historian Carolyn Merchant called my attention to this parallelism. She describes the death of nature as the event that turned not only the concept but the very experience of the universe in Western tradition topsy-turvy. She finds a motif—the aliveness of nature—common to all schools of philosophy since the time of the pre-Socratics. This motif found its expression in many versions, animist and hylo-morphist, idealist and gnostic. It is mirrored in innumerable proverbs and phrases. Well into the seventeenth century, the aliveness of nature is an axiomatic notion among all social levels.[6]

The word *nature* is derived from *nascitura*, which means "birthing," and nature is imagined and felt to be like a pregnant womb, a matrix, a mother; *natura a nascitura dicitur.* In its aliveness, nature brings forth both lifeless and living beings. Woman's pregnancy is the eminent analogy to nature's constant action. From Augustine to the high Middle Ages, pagan nature was baptized and progressively Christianized. It acquired a transcendent character without losing its way of being and its mode of action as a matrix. Here, the whole of nature is conceived as a reality deriving its being and aliveness from a transcendent source. Nature's aliveness and pregnancy are rooted in the continual creative activity of God. The world becomes a gift. Nature engenders insofar as it is sustained and elevated by the hand of God. The technical word for this ontic anchorage of being and becoming, of all nature, in God who is Life, is *contingency.* This term means that the aliveness of nature is experienced as the result of its "closeness" to the Creator. Nature's aliveness is an outgrowth of that Life which God is and which finds its expression in innumerable shades of being alive, but differently in mud and gems, salvia plants and cedars of Lebanon, stars and woman. And there are corresponding differences in contingency.

According to Merchant, the adventure of modern thought can be seen as the struggle to disentangle nature from its contingency, to sever its aliveness from the life of God. And, through this disentanglement, nature has been doubly redefined. It has lost not only its (Christian) contingency, but also its cosmic Greek aliveness. Giordano Bruno uproots the cosmos ontically when he follows Copernicus and pushes the earth out of the center of the cosmos. He takes the world out of the hand of God and thereby faces God with the world as his correlate. Bruno does this beautifully in his Oxford lectures, where he speaks of the cosmos as an organism of orderly worlds. Henceforth, nature is the order of things and only metaphorically still referred to as a matrix. Descartes takes the next step in the disembedding of things. For him, each thing has its own nature, and its existence rests on its entitlement to be according to its nature.

With this process, called "the death of Nature" by Merchant, a gnawing new but frequently suppressed question orients thought about living beings: how do we explain the existence of living forms in a dead cosmos? Nature has ceased to percolate in the old way and must rest in itself rather than in the hands of the Creator. If some things are alive, they now stand in a different opposition to other things that are not. If this is so, their aliveness can either be reduced to a peculiar process or else "something" must be postulated to explain it.

It would be superficial to explain the concept of substantive life as a direct answer to the above question. But it is fruitless to discuss the fascination of life for both clergymen and advertising moguls without keeping "the fading of nature as living matrix" present in one's mind. This is particularly so for one who would try to understand the mood of the present. Only in a cultural milieu where nature has been experienced for a couple of millennia as a pregnant womb can the death of nature be experienced as existential loneliness. With the death of nature, all things—from soil to beast, from the earth's attraction to a child's babble—lose the transcendent aliveness which had always been an integral aspect of their being. All things acquire the factualness characteristic of modernity; the fetus appears as "a fact" in woman's womb.

Understanding modernity as a result of this loss, one can begin to see why those who feel responsible conjure up the empty idol, "life."

17

The Blue Disk and the Pink Disk

꙰ IN MY OFFICE, books dealing with the fetus fill two large bookshelves. On one shelf, the fetus is a challenge to the engineer, on the other, to the moralist. The outpouring of the respective discourses floods the terrain where I do my historical groundwork on the fetus, all that remains after the death of nature. Like nature, each womb has been transformed into a field of operations. The bubbling and quickening beneath the heart of women has been turned into a public spectacle. And the way this show is watched, reported, protected, and its supply lines managed reinforces this perception of the fetus as one of the central things left behind after the death of nature. The *secreta mulierum* are laid out like any estate that can be inspected and, after deliberation, improved. Most embarrassingly, this is not "just" something being done to women. More important, perhaps, it mirrors their acquisition of a new consciousness.

But the womb is not only shamelessly exposed to researchers, administrators, and concerned neighbors across the street; it has also become the site of a new cathedral. Parliamentarians in the Bundestag, Baptists from the American South, the Pope in Rome, and a sundry collection of other guardians of morals all seem to agree that the contents of the womb are sacred. To understand this use of language, it is necessary to go beyond the vocabulary of biology, law, and—in a way—even philosophy and analyze that aspect of the womb's contents for which sacredness is claimed. By the common agreement of otherwise incompatible factions, something transcending natural facticity manifests and morally imposes itself through the appearance of a fetus in the womb.

The full force of this claim cannot be appropriately cast in a language that limits itself to the concepts of semantics or symbolic anthropology. The one discipline that can perhaps help us is religious science. By using concepts shaped within this admittedly hybrid field of discourse, it is possible to go beyond my previous insight showing the fetus to be the *objectum nostri temporis,* the paradigmatic or ideal object of our time, and reveal it also as the modern *sacrum.*

According to Mircea Eliade, the *sacrum* or *to hieron* is that object in which the transcendent appears. It is a technical term for those things to which the manifestation is tied. The quality and form in which the sacred can be experienced know no limits, but a *sacrum,* a material object, will always be found at the center of culture. In, through, or around this object, the culture's hierophany takes place. Here, the rootedness of reality in the beyond can be experienced. Here, the embeddedness of everyday experience in another dimension can be celebrated. The *sacrum* can be a rock or a tree, a mountain or a man, a fountain or a food. It is always a thing, a here and a there. For this reason, *to heiron* is neither image nor likeness, neither symbol nor metaphor; it is threshold rather than arrow. It is a frontier at which one can wait, a doorway to the beyond, a window.[1] Several anthropologists have accepted Eliade's ideas, some postulating a *sacrum* as a necessary condition for the existence of a culture. They argue that a society rests on the existence of normative assumptions that are neither right nor wrong, true nor untrue. These assumptions appear categorically in the *sacrum* without losing their transcendence, and it is this latter which vouches for their validity here and on the other side. The place or thing which roots the appearance of *to hieron* in the cultural universe is precisely the *sacrum.*

In modern society we are not accustomed to ascribing a religious character to foundational certainties that reach beyond the horizon of everyday experience. No one takes the inscription "In God We Trust" on the dollar bill seriously, while some through the Constitutional exorcism of the First Amendment carefully guard all children from any official celebration of transcendence. But these characteristics of our time do not deter me in my search for the modern *sacrum.* Precisely at the moment of unacknowledged decline, the American republic needs a *sacrum* more credible than its flag. And what would be better for this purpose than the American womb? I cannot think of a more straight-forward explanation for the obsessive attribution of life to a fetus than to see in it the hierophany of a secular dream about flesh reduced to an object.

The fetus that turned into a welcome neoplasm for Joanne is the emphatic embodiment of a scientifically generated fact. For her mother, perhaps, nature still conjured up something of a living matrix, and in that sense the stirring in her was part of nature's aliveness. For Joanne, however, the sonogram establishes a fact, which she names John. For Susan, the same fact is the *sacrum* in which a life appears wherever she is shown the emblem of the fetus—on a billboard, inside a balloon, or next to her coffee cup on the table.

I expect immediate criticism from anyone familiar with the current use of the term *sacrum* in the religious sciences. The *sacrum*, almost by definition, has always been a thing, not its shadow, an aura, an emana-tion, or an illusion. If the fetus is the *sacrum* of our time, it is a *sacrum* of a new kind. In our world, where we increasingly live not among things we see but among appearances we are shown, the modern *sacrum* also has the character of a media event.

Susan, like Joanne, looks at a test result. Joanne sees it as a baby, Susan, perhaps, as a new immune system. Weeks ago, a chemical test showed that a new biochemical process had begun, regulated by a program distinct from the mother's. In the mother's system, a new parasitical system has become nested. A fetus is organizing itself within the field of the mother. More and more, it is viewed primarily as a new cybernetic state that can take the form of a zygote, embryo, or child. That, roughly, is what is being drilled into Susan in biology class, where she explores this process on its different levels through a teach-ing machine equipped with hypertext.

But Susan cannot live with the fetus simply as an abstract construct of systems theory. In her fantasy, she transforms the dynamic equilib-rium of that open process into a "something." By hook or by crook, she imputes some meaning, some sense, to the formula. She names the cybernetic process "a life." And that life needs to be somewhere. Susan is too well trained to conceive of the womb romantically as a nest for Nilsson's creatures. The reduction of the uterine event to the level of an immune subsystem has extinguished the womb's sensual charac-teristics and transformed it into a digital desert. Sprouting in this digital desert, the fetus reveals itself to Susan as "life."

The public fetus functions as an emblem for Joanne, an idol for Susan. The emblem provides a normative interpretation of biological events, the idol, a threshold where Susan worships a misunderstanding engendered by pop-science.

It would be silly to consider this idolatry of life a consequence of noisy disputes about Supreme Court decisions, Constitutional amendments, and congressional proposals. The growing ecumenical consensus about the sacredness of life is better understood as an aspect of a surreptitious shift in social and medical management concerns about the importance of "survival." Twenty years ago, Erich Fromm pointed out the necrophiliac intensity that emanates from this word.[2] Joy in the aliveness of nature, of the lily, the lark, and the infant, no longer motivates those who use this terrible word, but rather, fear, calculation, and something Freimut Duve (another German colleague) calls "apocalyptic randiness."

The idol of the fetus has only one competitor at present, and that is the Blue Planet. Just as the sonogram of the fetus stands for one life, so the TV satellite picture of the earth stands for all life. As the pink disk of the zygote appeals for the maintenance of one immune system, so the blue disk of the biosphere appeals for the survival of the entire global system.[3] Both disks act like sacraments for the "real presence" of life, for whose continuation a global "we" is made responsible. Thus, a misplaced concreteness, which makes the fetus into an object, creates the *sacrum* in which the futile pursuit of survival overpowers contemporary consciousness. As I have said, curiosity thrust me into the study of the history of pregnancy. I wanted to find out if I could experience myself other than through contemporary certainties. My excursions into Eisenach, to the Tailor's Wife whose stagnations are alien and repellent to me, encouraged me to take a stand that I would also wish for my friends: to ruefully smile at this phantom. Then one can speak an unconditional NO to life, recovering one's own autonomous aliveness.

\

Notes

Introduction

1. *Gott ist ein Freund des Lebens: Herausforderungen und Aufgaben beim Schutz des Lebens* (Trier: Paulinus Verlag, 1989), pp. 11, 29.

2. *Frankfurter Allgemeine Zeitung,* April 5, 1991. The speech of Cardinal Ratzinger on the "Problem of the Threat to Life" can be found in *L'Osservatore Romano,* April 16, 1991.

3. Raymond Williams, *Key Words: A Vocabulary of Culture and Society* (New York: Oxford University Press, 1976).

4. The challenge that led me to several years' work on the "history of the unborn" came from two friends, Susanne von Paczenski and Renate Sadrozinski. For a long time I have admired their efforts to put the feelings and status of women with unwanted pregnancies into the center of public discussion about women in Germany. Susanne von Paczenski, *Gemischte Gefühle: Von Frauen, die ungewollte schwanger sind* (Munich: Beck Verlag, 1987); and Susanne von Paczenski and Renate Sadrozinski, eds., *Paragraph 218: Zu Lasten der Frauen* (Reinbek: Rowohlt Verlag, 1988).

1. The Lost Horizon

1. Michel Foucault, *The Use of Pleasure,* vol. 2 of *The History of Sexuality,* trans. Robert Hurley (New York: Pantheon, 1985), pp. 8f.

2. Caroline Bynum, *Holy Feast and Holy Fast: The Religious Significance of Food to Medieval Women* (Berkeley: University of California Press, 1987); Marie-Christine Pouchelle, *Corps et chirurgie à l'apogée du Moyen Age* (Paris: Flammarion, 1983) (an English translation exists); Ludmilla Jordanova, *Sexual Visions: Images of Gender in Science and Medicine between the Eighteenth and Twentieth Century* (Madison, Wis.: University of Wisconsin Press, 1989); Emily Martin, *The Woman in the Body: A Cultural Analysis of Reproduction* (Boston:

Beacon Press, 1987); Angus McLaren, *Reproductive Rituals: The Perception of Fertility in England from the Sixteenth to the Nineteenth Century* (New York: Methuen, 1984); Thomas Laqueur, *Making Sex: Body and Gender from the Greeks to Freud* (Cambridge, Mass.: Harvard University Press, 1990).

3. Giulia Sissa, *Greek Virginity*, trans. Arthur Goldhammer (Cambridge, Mass.: Harvard University Press, 1990); Aline Rousselle, *Porneia: On Desire and the Body in Antiquity*, trans. Felicia Pheasant (London: Basil Blackwell, 1988); Peter Brown, *The Body and Society: Men, Women and Sexual Renunciation in Early Christianity* (New York: Columbia University Press, 1988).

4. *ME'AM LO'EZ: El Gran Comentario Biblico Sefardi. Bereshit* (Madrid: Gredos, 1969). This is a Latin alphabet edition of the original published in Istanbul in 1730.

5. Questions of this kind have been raised and explored by Sarah Franklin, "Fetal Fascinations: New Dimensions to the Medical-scientific Construction of Fetal Personhood," in Sarah Franklin, Celia Lury, Jackey Stacey, eds., *Off-Centre: Feminism and Cultural Studies* (London: Harper Collins Academic, 1991), pp. 19–205; Sarah Franklin, "Life Story: The Gene as Fetish Object on TV," *Science as Culture* 3 (1988):92–100. I came to know her writings only after I had written this English version of *Der Frauenleib als öffentlicher Ort*, and I was therefore unable to draw on her insights into the graphic representation of what she calls "fetal teleologies."

6. Barbara Duden, *The Woman beneath the Skin: A Doctor's Patients in Eighteenth-Century Germany*, trans. Thomas Dunlap (Cambridge, Mass.: Harvard University Press, 1991).

2. The Nilsson Effect

1. *Life*, April 30, 1965 (cover).

2. *Life*, April 30, 1965 (story). In these stories gendered "subjectivity" is imputed to egg and sperm. A fine analysis is given by Emily Martin, "The Egg and the Sperm: How Science Has Constructed a Romance Based on Stereotypical Male-Female Roles," *Signs* 16, 3 (1991): 485–501.

3. *Life*, August 1990 (cover and headlines).

4. *Der Stern*, September 6, 1990, p. 44.

5. Marjorie Nicolson, *Science and Imagination* (Ithaca: Cornell University Press, 1956), pp. 165 ff. vividly describes Leeuwenhoek's curiosity and his impact on people's perception. Clifford Dobell, *Antony van Leeuwenhoek and His "Little Animals"* (New York: Russell & Russell, 1932) is still the best introduction.

6. Roland Barthes, *Camera Lucida: Reflections on Photography*, trans. Richard Howard (New York: Hill and Wang, 1981).

7. Susan Sontag, *On Photography* (New York: Farrar, Straus and Giroux, 1989), p. 5.

8. Joseph Cardinal Ratzinger, "Instruction on Respect for Human Life in Its

Origin and on the Dignity of Procreation," *Orogons*, March 19, 1987, p. 107. This is the official Vatican English translation.

9. Ibid., p. 701.

10. *Constitutio de Fide Catolica*, 4. Found in H. Denzinger, *Enchiridion symbolorum et definitionum*, no. 1785.

11. Ratzinger, "Instruction," p. 710.

12. Joseph Ratzinger, *Christian Brotherhood* (London: Sheed and Ward, 1966).

13. Ratzinger, "Instruction," p. 701.

14. Ibid.

3. The Average Fetus in Harlem

1. See Rayna Rapp, "Chromosomes and Communication: The Discourse of Genetic Counseling," *Medical Anthropology Quarterly* 2 (1988): 143–157; and "Women, Men and Fetuses on a Frontier of Reproductive Technologies," *Women and Health* 13 (1988): 101–116, which analyze genetic counseling in New York. Rapp recognizes the depth to which intense social control colonizes the mind of women, but believes they could be "informed" without being victimized by diagnosis.

2. See "Population," in *The Development Dictionary: A Guide to Knowledge as Power*, ed. Wolfgang Sachs (London: Zed Books, 1992), pp. 146–157. Here, I analyze the notion of population, both born and fetal, within the development discourse. I found that around 1972, the graphic representation of population statistics switches from bar-graph to flow-chart, and the text begins to deal with "populations" as a dependent variable within the development formula. I liken this conceptual shift to an epistemic extermination. See also Herbert Mehrtens, "Verantwortungslose Reinheit: Thesen zur politischen und moralischen Struktur mathematischer Wissenschaften am Beispiel des NS-Staates," in Georges Fulgras and Annegret Falter, eds., *Wissenschaft in der Verantwortung: Möglichkeiten der institutionellen Steuerung* (Frankfurt-am-Main: Campus, 1990), pp. 37–54; and William Arney, *Power and the Profession of Obstetrics* (Chicago: University of Chicago Press, 1982), pp. 134 ff.

4. Joanne and Susan

1. Stanley Joel Reiser, *Medicine and the Reign of Technology* (Cambridge: Cambridge University Press, 1978), pp. 23–44.

2. Ann Oakley, *Captured Womb: A History of Medical Care of Pregnant Women* (Oxford: Blackwell, 1984), pp. 155–186, describes the history of technological innovations in prenatal care; she stresses the importance that visualization has had on pregnant women's self-perception. See also her article, "From Walking Wombs to Test-Tube Babies," in *Reproductive Technologies*, ed. Michelle Stanworth (Minneapolis: University of Minnesota Press, 1987), pp. 36–56.

5. How the Body Became a Showcase

1. Hildegard of Bingen, *Heilkunde: Liber causae et curiae,* trans. Heinrich Schipperges (Salzburg: Otto Müller, 1957), p. 130 (Chap. 6).

2. *ME'AM LO'EZ: El Gran Comentario Biblico Sefardi. Bereshit* (Madrid: Gredos, 1969), p. 140.

3. Anatomical Fugitive Sheet: Jobst de Negker, "Anathomia oder Abconterfettung eines Weibs Leib," (Augsburg, 1538; Strasbourg, 1544). Reproduced in Robert Herrlinger, *Geschichte der medizinischen Abbildung. I: Von der Antike bis um 1600* (Munich: Heinz Moos Verlag, 1967), p. 165. There is an English translation.

4. Quoted in L. Heydenreich, *Leonardo da Vinci* (London: Macmillan, 1954), p. 123.

5. In my approach to the printed picture as mindshaping device I owe much to William Ivins, the former curator of graphic arts at the Metropolitan Museum of Art in New York. See "The Blocked Road to Pictorial Communication," the first chapter in his *Prints and Visual Communication* (Cambridge, Mass.: Harvard University Press, 1953), pp. 1–20.

6. Quoted in Michael Sukale, ed., *Sehen als Erkennen: Leonardo Da Vincis Zeichnungen in Faksimile* (Constanz: University of Constanz Library, 1987), p. 74.

7. William Hunter, Preface to *Anatomia uteri humani gravidi. The anatomy of the human gravid uterus* (Birmingham: Baskerville, 1774). For a comparison with other contemporary anatomical atlases, see Ludmilla Jordanova, "Gender, Generation and Science: William Hunter's Obstetrical Atlas," in *William Hunter and the Eighteenth-Century Medical World,* ed. W. F. Bynum and R. Porter (Cambridge: Cambridge University Press, 1985), pp. 385–412.

8. Hunter, Preface to *Anatomia.*

9. Ibid.

10. Quoted in Kenneth Keele, *Leonardo da Vinci's Elements of the Science of Man* (San Diego: Academic Press, 1983), p. 197.

11. Hunter, Preface to *Anatomia.*

12. Samuel Thomas Soemmering, *Abbildungen und Beschreibungen einiger Missgeburten, die sich ehemals auf dem Anatomischen Theater zu Cassel befanden* (Mainz, 1791), p. 5.

13. Ibid.

14. Samuel Thomas Soemmering, Preface to *Icones Embryonum Humanorum* (Frankfurt-am-Main, 1799), p. 2.

15. Ibid.

16. Soemmering, *Icones,* Explicatio Tab. I, p. 5.

6. A Skeptical Discipline

1. K. D. Keele and C. Pedretti, *Leonardo da Vinci: Corpus of the Anatomical Studies in the Collection of Her Majesty the Queen at Windsor Castle* (London: Johnson Reprint Company, 1979), no. 112 r.

2. *The Illustrations from the Works of Andreas Vesalius of Brussels,* annotated and translated by J. B. de C. M. Saunders and Charles D. O'Malley (New York: Dover, 1950), Plates 21–37.

3. Fabricius, Letter of Dedication in *De formato foetu* (Venedig, 1600). Facsimile and translation in *The Embryological Treatises of Hiernonymus Fabricius of Aquapendente,* trans. Howard B. Adelmann (Ithaca: Cornell University Press, 1942), p. 237.

4. Fabricius, *De formato foetu,* Table III, reprinted in Adelmann, *Embryological Treatises.*

7. The Public Fetus

1. Rosalind Petchesky, "Fetal Images: The Power of Visual Culture in the Politics of Reproduction," *Feminist Studies* 13, 2 (1987): 263–292: "the fetal personhood [becomes] a self-fulfilling prophecy by making the fetus a public presence [that] addresses a visually oriented culture" (p. 264).

2. Eva Schindele, *Gläserne Gebär-Mutter: Vorgeburtliche Diagnostik: Fluch oder Segen* (Frankfurt-am-Main: Fischer Verlag, 1990).

3. "Sezieren," *Deutsches Fremdwörterbuch,* ed. Hans Schulz (Strasbourg: Trübner, 1974).

8. The Legal Status of the Not-Yet

1. Aristotle, *Generation of Animals,* II. IV (739b, 21–25), trans. A. L. Peck (Cambridge, Mass.: Harvard University Press, 1942).

2. Hildegard of Bingen, *Wisse die Wege: Scivias,* trans. Maura Böckeler (Salzburg: Otto Müller, 1984), p. 27 (Vision four: 13).

3. Hippocrates, *De natura pueri,* XII, 4–5, in *The Hippocratic Treatises "On Generation," "On the Nature of the Child,"* ed. Iain Lonie (Berlin: De Gruyter, 1982): "the seed is made warm by the warmth of its environment . . . as it inflates, the seed forms a membrane around itself . . . in just the same way a thin membrane is formed on the surface of bread when it is being baked: the bread rises as it grows warm and inflates" (pp. 6–7).

4. Quoted in Danielle Jacquart and Claude Thomasset, *Sexualité et savoir medical au Moyen Age* (Paris: Presses Universitaires de France, 1985), p. 32.

5. Ibid., p. 86.

6. Jan Swammerdam, *Miraculum naturae sive uteri muliebris fabrica* (Leiden, 1672), p. 19.

7. See Esther Fischer-Homberger, *Medizin vor Gericht: Gerichtsmedizin von der Renaissance bis zur Aufklärung* (Bern/Stuttgart: Verlag Hans Huber, 1983), pp. 222–244.

8. For the history of the law, see John T. Noonan, Jr., ed., *The Morality of Abortion: Legal and Historical Perspectives* (Cambridge, Mass.: Harvard University Press, 1970); W. J. Curran, "An Historical Perspective on the Law of Personality and Status with Special Regard to the Human Fetus and the Rights

of Women," *Health and Science: Milbank Memorial Fund Quarterly* 61, 1 (1983): 58–67.

9. John T. Noonan, Jr., "An Almost Absolute Value in History," in Noonan, *The Morality of Abortion,* p. 20.

10. Günter Jerouschek, *Lebensschutz und Lebensbeginn: Kulturgeschichte des Abtreibungsverbots* (Stuttgart: Enke, 1988).

11. Angus McLaren, *Reproductive Rituals: The Perception of Fertility in England from the Sixteenth to the Nineteenth Century* (London: Methuen, 1984), Chap. 5, "Converting this Measure of Security into a Crime": "As a consequence, actions traditionally not subjected to prosecution were now declared to be criminal although in practice only when carried out by nonmedical personnel . . . Doctors had accomplished the remarkable feat of creating a taboo which they alone could freely violate" (p. 143).

12. J. Mangan, S. J., "The Wonder of Myself: Ethical-Theological Aspects of Direct Abortion," *Theological Studies* 31, 1 (1970): 128–148. On pages 141 ff. he describes the steps in the formation of the "immediate-hominization theory" that paralleled the genesis of scientific cell theory. In 1869, Pius IX eliminated the distinction between the animated and the unanimated fetus as far as the penalty of excommunication was concerned. Toward the end of the century, in 1884, 1889, 1895, and 1898, "the Holy Office . . . made it explicitly clear that . . . all direct expulsion of nonviable fetuses . . . [is] morally wrong and admit[s] no exceptions" (p. 144). "The fetus from the first moment of conception theologically must be baptized and must be treated as a human person" (p. 144). This is taken from a standard manual of moral theology of the time, Vermeersch, *Theologia moralis.*

9. The Tailor's Wife

1. Barbara Duden, *The Woman beneath the Skin: A Doctor's Patients in Eighteenth-Century Germany,* trans. Thomas Dunlop (Cambridge, Mass.: Harvard University Press, 1991).

2. Johann Storch, *Von Weiberkrankheiten, 4. Bandes, I. Teil, darinnen vornehmlich solche Zufälle, welche Molas oder Muttergewächse und falsche Früchte betreffen* (*Diseases of Women,* vol. 4, part 1, wherein primarily such mishaps as concern lumps or womb growth and false fruits are discussed) (Gotha, 1749), case 19, pp. 100–101.

3. Johann Storch, *Von Weiberkrankheiten, 4. Bandes, II. Teil, vom Abortu oder Missfall* (*Diseases of Women,* vol. 4, part 2, of abortions or miscarriages) (Gotha, 1749), pp. 11 ff.

4. Ibid., pp. 224 ff.

10. The Thought Collective and the Construction of Reality

1. Ludwik Fleck, *Genesis and Development of a Scientific Fact,* ed. Th. Trenn and R. K. Merton (Chicago: University of Chicago Press, 1979).

2. Ludwik Fleck, "On the Crisis of 'Reality'," in *Cognition and Fact—Mate-*

rials on Ludwik Fleck, ed. R. S. Cohen and T. Schnelle (Dordrecht: Reidel, 1986), pp. 47–57. The quote occurs on p. 53.

3. Ibid., p. 53.

4. *Das Leben des ungeborenen Kindes*, ed. Sekretariat der Deutschen Bischofskonferenz (Bonn, 1986), (Arbeitshilfen 48), p. 5.

11. The Neo-plasm in the Entrails

1. Personal conversation.

2. Uwe Pörksen, *Plastikwörter: Die Sprache einer internationalen Diktatur* (Stuttgart: Klett-Cotta, 1988). A short version of Pörksen's argument can be found in his article "Scientific and Mathematical Colonization of Colloquial Language," *Rivista di Biologia* 81, 3 (1988): 381–400.

3. *Süddeutsche Zeitung*, Magazin, July 6, 1990, p. 17.

12. Quickening and the King's Mistress

1. *The Diary of Samuel Pepys*, ed. Robert Latham and William Matthews (Berkeley: University of California Press, 1971), vol. 4, p. 1.

2. Martin Lechner, *Maria Gravida: Zum Schwangerschaftsmotiv in der Bildenden Kunst* (Munich: Schnell-Steiner, 1981).

3. Bernard Nathanson, *Aborting America* (New York: Doubleday, 1979), p. 206.

4. William Blackstone, *Commentaries on the Laws of England* (London: n.p., 1765), vol. 1, p. 129.

5. Angus McLaren, *Reproductive Rituals: The Perception of Fertility in England from the Sixteenth to the Nineteenth Century* (London: Methuen, 1984), p. 138.

6. James Mohr, *Abortion in America: The Origins and Evolution of National Policy, 1800–1900* (New York: Oxford University Press, 1978), p. 4.

7. Carol Smith-Rosenberg, "The Abortion Movement and the AMA, 1850–1880," in Carol Smith-Rosenberg, *Disorderly Conduct: Visions of Gender in Victorian America* (New York: Knopf, 1985), pp. 217–244.

13. Fluxes and Stagnations

1. Johann Storch, *Krankheiten der Weiber, dritter Band, darinnen vornehmlich solche casus, welche die Schwangeren betreffen* (Diseases of Women, vol. 3, wherein primarily such cases as concern pregnant women are discussed) (Gotha, 1748), pp. 508–509.

2. Dorothy Porter and Roy Porter, *Patient's Progress: Doctors and Doctoring in Eighteenth-century England* (Oxford: Blackwell, 1989); *The Diary of Ralph Josselin (1616–1683)*, ed. Alan MacFarlane (London: Oxford University Press, 1976); Lucy M. Beier, *Sufferers and Healers: The Experience of Illness in Seventeenth-Century England* (London: Routledge and Kegan Paul, 1987), pp. 146 ff.

3. Rudolf zur Lippe, *Naturbeherrschung am Menschen: Geometrisierung des*

Menschen und Repräsentation des Privaten im Französischen Absolutismus, vol. 2 (Frankfurt-am-Main: Syndikat Verlag, 1981).

4. Marie-Christine Pouchelle, *Corps et Chirurgie à l'apogée du Moyen Age* (Paris: Flammarion, 1983), pp. 224–227.

5. Grete Luers, *Die Sprache der deutschen Mystik des Mittelalters im Werke der Mechthild von Magdeburg* (Munich: Einhard, 1926); Carolyn Walker Bynum, *Jesus as Mother: Studies in the Spirituality of the High Middle Ages* (Berkeley: University of California Press, 1982), Chaps. 4ff.

6. *Hildegard of Bingen's Scivias,* trans. Bruce Hozeski (Santa Fe, N.M.: Bear and Co., 1986), pp. 49 ff.

7. Hildegard of Bingen, *Heilkunde: Liber causae et curiae,* trans. Heinrich Schipperges (Salzburg: Otto Müller, 1957), p. 126.

8. Oswald Gabelkover, *Artzney-Buch: Darinnen fast für alle des Menschlichen Leibes Anliegen und Gebrechen ausserlesene und bewehrte Artzneyen,* 5th ed. (Frankfurt-am-Main, 1680), pp. 262–265.

14. Hapsis and Opsis

1. Rodney Needham, "Polithetic Classification: Convergence and Consequences," *Man,* n.s. 10, no. 3 (Sept. 1975): 349–369.

2. Marie-Christine Pouchelle, *Corps et Chirurgie à l'apogée du Moyen Age* (Paris: Flammarion, 1983); Judith van Herik, "Simone Weil's Religious Imagery: How Looking Becomes Eating," in *Immaculate and Powerful: The Female in Sacred Image and Social Reality,* ed. Clarissa Atkinson (Boston: Beacon Press, 1985), pp. 260–282; Judith van Herik, "From Women's Words about Body to Freud's Words about Psyche: Notes on Disembedding Spirit from Flesh," manuscript (Cambridge, Mass.: Harvard Divinity School, March 15, 1990).

3. Arthur Kutzelnigg, "Die Verarmung des Geruchswortschatzes seit dem Mittelalter," *Muttersprache* 94, nos. 3–4 (1983–84): 328–345.

15. The Uterine Police

1. These cases are taken from Richard van Dülmen, *Frauen vor Gericht: Kindsmord in der Frühen Neuzeit* (Frankfurt-am-Main: Fischer Verlag, 1991).

2. Wilhelm Gottfried Ploucquet, *Abhandlung über die gewaltsamen Todesarten,* 2nd ed. (Tübingen, 1788), p. 246.

3. Ibid., pp. 235 ff.

4. Ibid., p. 242.

5. Ibid., p. 255.

6. Ibid., p. 263.

16. Synthetic Life

1. See the chapter, "The Institutional Construction of a new Fetish: Human Life," in Ivan Illich, *In the Mirror of the Past: Lectures and Addresses 1978–1990* (London: Marion Boyars, 1992), pp. 218–231; Chap. 10, "A Cosmos in the

Hands of Man," in David Cayley, *Ivan Illich in Conversation* (Toronto: Anansi, 1992), pp. 252–288.

2. *Gott ist ein Freund des Lebens: Herausforderungen und Aufgaben beim Schutz des Lebens* (Trier: Paulinus Verlag, 1989), p. 104.

3. Dirk von Boetticher, who studied medicine and philosophy together for several years, has called my attention to the implications of my studies on the body of woman for the concept of "life" in the history of ideas.

4. James Lovelock, *Gaia: A New Look at Life on Earth* (Oxford: Oxford University Press, 1987).

5. Donald Worster, *Nature's Economy: A History of Ecological Ideas* (Cambridge: Cambridge University Press, 1985); Wolfgang Sachs, "Environment," in *The Development Dictionary: A Guide to Knowledge as Power*, ed. Wolfgang Sachs (London: Zed Books, 1992), pp. 26–37; Wolfgang Sachs, "Natur als System: Vorläufiges zu einer Kritik der Ökologie," *Scheidewege: Jahresschrift für skeptisches Denken* 21 (1991/92): 83–97.

6. Carolyn Merchant, *Death of Nature: Women, Ecology and the Scientific Revolution* (New York: Harper and Row, 1983).

17. The Blue Disk and the Pink Disk

1. Mircea Eliade, *The Sacred and the Profane: The Nature of Religion* (Magnolia, Mass.: Peter Smith, 1959).

2. Erich Fromm, in conversation, while preparing his *For the Love of Life* (New York: Free Press, 1986).

3. The ambiguity of this symbol, which stands for both "system" and control and evokes the threat to *"Heimat,"* is central for the "epistemology of ecology" on which Wolfgang Sachs is working. See his "One World" in *The Development Dictionary: A Guide to Knowledge as Power* (London: Zed Books, 1992), pp. 102–114; and his "Satellitenblick: Die Visualisierung der Erde im Zuge der Weltraumfahrt," manuscript (Berlin: Wissenschaftszentrum Berlin, 1992).

Index

Abortion, 3, 4, 28, 50, 54, 64, 65, 76;
legal/religious views of, 21, 59–60, 82;
as infanticide, 60; therapeutic, 60;
criminalization of, 82
abortus, 65
Age of mother, 26–27, 31
Amenorrhea, 87, 94. *See also*
Menstruation
American Medical Association, 82
"Amoeba words," 74–75
Anatomia uteri gravidi (Hunter's atlas),
34, 39, 40, 47
Anatomists, 3, 38, 39, 40–42, 45, 68
Anatomy, development of, 45
animalcula seminalia, 15
Angels, 9
Aristotle, 45, 56, 58, 71, 102–103
Art, the unborn in, 16, 32, 34–42,
46–47, 79–80. *See also* Engraving;
Photography
Artist, vs. anatomist, 37, 40–41
Atomistic view, 48
Autopsy, 37. *See also* Dissection

Baptism, 61
Barthes, Roland, 19
Beauty, 41–42
Berlin Wall, 17
Bio-bias, 52, 81
Biology, 103
Blackstone, William, 59, 82

Bloodletting, 84, 87–88
Blue Planet, 2, 10, 17, 100, 110
Body, 6–7, 49; as transparent, 48, 49;
metaphors for, 85–86
Body history, 3, 8, 44, 85–86, 91
Boetticher, Dirk von, 102
Book of Job, 56–57
Brandt, Susanna Margaretha, 94–95
Brotherhood, concept of, 22–24
Bruno, Giordano, 104
Burdach, K. F., 103
Bynum, Carolyn, 6, 86

Cangiamilia, Reverend, 53
Catholicism, 1–2, 21–24, 59–60, 61, 82.
See also Christianity; Churches
Chargaff, Erwin, 71
Charles V, 60
"Cheese making," womb as vessel for,
56–57, 58
Christianity, 23–24, 60–61, 79–80, 102.
See also Catholicism; Churches
Churches: view on life, 1–2, 21–24,
59–61, 69, 70, 101, 102; view on
abortion, 21, 59–60, 82; and
ensoulment, 60–61, 103. *See also*
Catholicism; Christianity
Clotting, 86–87
Common law, 82, 101
Conception, 11, 12–14, 18
Concreteness, misplaced, 20, 23, 25